D1613340

Playing for RANGERS No. 3

Overleaf: **A glimpse of the action around the Bayern Munich goal at Ibrox in the second leg Fairs Cup tie. The West German international goalkeeper Sepp Maier races for the ball, challenged by Rangers' striker Colin Stein, backed up by teenager Derek Johnstone.**

**Edited by
KEN GALLACHER**

**Stanley Paul
London**

Playing for RANGERS No. 3

STANLEY PAUL & CO LTD
3 Fitzroy Square, London W1

AN IMPRINT OF THE HUTCHINSON GROUP

London Melbourne Sydney
Auckland Johannesburg Cape Town
and agencies throughout the world
First published 1971

*This book has been set in Baskerville, printed in Great Britain
by offset litho at Flarepath Printers Ltd., Colney Street, St. Albans, Herts.
and bound by William Brendon, at Tiptree, Essex*

ISBN 0 09 108340 0

Contents

RANGERS F.C. 1970/71

Back row: **(Left to Right) A. Conn, C. Stein, G. Donaldson, G. Neef, P. McCloy, C. Jackson, B. Watson, D. Stevenson, N. Stevenson, G. Fyfe, I. MacDonald.**

Middle row: **(Left to Right) J. Wallace (Coach), T. Craig (Physio.), K. Watson, W. Mathieson, D. Renton, R. McKinnon, A. Miller, S. Jardine, D. Johnstone, D. Smith, A. McCallum, J. Craven (assist. Trainer), S. Anderson (Trainer).**

Front row: **(Left to Right) W. Waddell (Manager), W. Henderson, W. Semple, A. MacDonald, T. Alexander, J. Greig, D. Parlane, A. Penman, A. Morrison, W. Johnston, W. Thornton (Assist. Manager).**

TOMMY McLEAN

Rangers....
My Dream Club

IT MAY SEEM strange to many football fans in Scotland when I tell them now that it has always been my ambition to join Rangers, that the Ibrox club has always been the greatest club in the world as far as I am concerned . . . but it is true.

The reason why it will seem strange is simple. You see, back when I was leaving school and was just fifteen years old I turned down the chance to sign for Rangers. I had the opportunity to go to Ibrox then and decided against it because I was persuaded that I would have a better chance at Kilmarnock. And the man who was so persuasive that night nine years ago was Mr. Willie Waddell, the present Rangers' manager who signed me for the second time last summer!

I can still remember that night so vividly. Both Mr. Waddell and the Rangers' Manager, at that time, Mr Scot Symon, were at the house on the same night. Both were wanting me to sign and even though I admired Rangers so much I went to Rugby Park. Mr. Waddell impressed me so much then. He pointed out that he would give me advice and guidance on and off the field and that I would be going straight into his reserve team. There would be no delaying over my playing senior football . . . he wanted me in the reserves and he wanted me playing regularly and that's what eventually convinced me that I would have a better chance of making the grade with Killie.

It took a lot to turn down Rangers but I weighed everything up very carefully that night. At Ibrox there was already a right wing battle going on between Willie Henderson and Alex Scott and I knew that it would be hard for me to get into the reserve team there. With Kilmarnock I was going to get that chance right away. . . .

Mr. Waddell kept his word and eventually he had a tremendous influence on my career. That's why, I suppose, I was so pleased when I learned that he wanted to sign me again . . . and this time, for the Rangers!

I was desperate to go to Ibrox by this time. Once before I had

9

Left: Tommy McLean

had the chance to move from Kilmarnock. When Tommy Docherty was the manager of Chelsea he made a bid of £90,000 for my transfer and it was accepted by the board of directors at Rugby Park. Somehow, though, going to England didn't appeal to me at that time and I refused the move to Stamford Bridge. There were times afterwards when I regretted it a little bit, but, not any more. Not now that I am with Rangers.

Anyhow, the Rangers tried very hard to sign me last season and twice the Kilmarnock directors rejected the bids that they had made for my transfer. I was upset by it all. I know that Rangers wanted me and I didn't hide the fact that this was the move that I wanted for myself. But it seemed to be deadlocked after the second bid was refused.

I felt terrible. I felt I was beginning to lose an interest in the game because I quite simply wasn't happy playing for Kilmarnock any more. I wanted to change clubs because I felt I was getting to a cross-roads in my own career. I had been with Killie for nine years and I'd managed to play in Europe with them, win Scottish international honours, but I knew that with a bigger club, a better club, that I could improve as a player. I wanted that so much.

At the start of June I was chosen as a member of Scotland's close-season touring squad and went to Denmark for the first match against the Danes in Copenhagen. My future looked bleak because Kilmarnock had stood firm on their decision and there appeared to have been no fresh moves from Ibrox.

But what I didn't know when I left was that Rangers had made a third offer which was to be discussed by Kilmarnock. This time it was accepted and I took part in a strange transfer . . . a transfer deal between two Scottish clubs which was carried out in Denmark.

Mr. Waddell and Kilmarnock's manager Mr. Walter McCrae flew out from Glasgow and came to the Scottish team's HQ at Vedbaek, a little fishing village on the outskirts of Copenhagen. They were given permission to see me and after talks I became a Rangers' player nine years after they first tried to sign me.

I felt tremendous. It was an ambition realised and I suppose that's why I hit form in the international the next night at the Idraetspark Stadium. Scotland lost the match, a European Nations Cup game, by 1-0 but the Danish journalists voted me their player of the game. I had really been bucked by the signing taking place. I mean, it had been so depressing before. So bad, in fact, that I even thought about quitting football. I was just fed-up playing for Kilmarnock.

Now, of course, all my old enthusiasm has returned. I feel as excited as I did when I was just setting out on my career as a fifteen years old schoolboy. You see, I know that Mr. Waddell will be looking after my career again, and he was always very fair to me at Kilmarnock. I remember that. I know, too, that I'll be playing for one of Europe's great clubs. There is a difference in playing for Kilmarnock or any of the other Scottish provincial clubs in Europe and playing for Rangers. Now I'm with a club which has built up a tremendous tradition and reputation right through the world. I am certain that this will help me in itself.

Also, I think I am going to be playing with better players at Ibrox, and again this is something which helps any player.

Most of all, though, I'll have the backing of the huge Ibrox support, the finest fans in the world. Instead of playing at Rugby Park in front of a few thousand fans, except when Rangers or Celtic go there, I'll have big crowds and any player will tell you how much inspiration that can provide.

All I want to do in my new career with Rangers is to provide value for the money that the club has paid for me. I don't want to start in a blaze of glory and then fade away. I don't want to have a few good games and then a whole lot of bad games. What I want to do is get consistency of performance and make sure that the good games I have for Rangers far out-number the bad games. That is my main ambition now. . . .

Because, you see, my other great ambition has been realised. I am a Rangers' player at last!

A glimpse into the dream that came true for Rangers' director David Hope with this picture of one of the main lounges in the half-a-million pounds' Social Club which was built for the fans.

The Fans' Blue Heaven
...and Beyond!

WHEN the Rangers' Social Club opened for the first time, an occasion marked by one of Glasgow's most glittering social occasions, a newspaper headline the next morning saluted the club as —'A Blue Heaven for the Fans'. And, really, it is difficult to move far from that headline when you try to sum up exactly what the club means to the diehard Rangers' fans who have become members.

It was close to disastrous that the club should be so severely damaged by fire just a month after the formal opening by Lord Provost Sir Donald Liddle of Glasgow ... damaged so extensively that it was closed for six months to have the repair work done.

Still, the intention of the repair work was to have the club looking as it did before the fire, and that means the 'Blue Heaven' tag will still fit so aptly.

The whole complex of the social club was the brainchild of Rangers' director David Hope and fittingly Hope is the man who runs the show there. It could be no other way. From the time that he first suggested a social club at Ibrox David Hope had a vision for the fans. A vision he brought to reality.

The day of the opening Hope spent eighteen hours at the club ensuring that everything would go smoothly. He says: 'I retired from my own business several years ago and was then invited by the Rangers' board to organise their pool. Now I find myself working harder than ever for the club . . . and enjoying every minute of it.

'I knew that when we were building a club for the Rangers' fans then it had to be the best. There was no way that it could be otherwise. Expense did not matter to us when the club was under construction and, naturally, it was the same when the repairs were being made. I wanted the best social club in the world for our fans and I think we succeeded in our aim.'

There were few of us who were there on that opening night who would be able to produce any kind of convincing argument against Hope. There was a luxurious touch to the club,

13

in the restaurants, in the lounges and in the superbly appointed committee room, discreetly lit and magnificently panelled. But this was the way that David Hope had wanted it. He admits: 'There are ideas incorporated from various clubs I have visited all over the world. Eventually we spent close to half-a-million pounds getting things done exactly the way we wanted them done.'

For Hope it is a totally new football world to the one he was born into. For this guiding spirit behind the pools and social club complex, this man who is used to having hundreds of thousands of pounds pouring through his hands can still tell you of his younger days in football. The days when he played as a goalkeeper for the Ashfield Intermediate team and junior team, when a signing on fee of £8 was something special and the negotiations were conducted, not in a lush club like the Ibrox one, but in an ice-cream shop in Saracen Street.

A view of part of the executive-styled dining room that Rangers' fans can use in their luxury Social Club . . .

Hope lives and breathes Glasgow's soccer lore. At times people get the wrong impression of this bustling director, they see only the business eyes, the side of Hope that organises the finances that help Rangers so much. They don't get the opportunity to see beyond that, to see the Hope who wants so desperately to see Rangers successful once again.

He tells you: 'I was asked to come out of retirement to do a job for the Rangers. I would never have left retirement to do it for anyone else, believe me. But because they asked me to organise the pools and then the social club I have directed all my energies towards these aspects of the club. Soon I hope that I will be helping to plan a new-look stadium where there will be many more seats available to the supporters.

'But before all of these things I want a great Rangers' team back out there on the field winning trophies again. I'm just like any of the fans as far as that is concerned. It will happen, 15 too, just wait and see.

'I have made predictions before. I predicted that the pools would grow to the present staggeringly high membership, and that some day we would have a social club to cater for the off-field activities of the fans. Now I have two more predictions. The first one is that we will have one of the best-equipped stadiums in the country inside the next few years. And the second is that under our Manager, Willie Waddell, Rangers will be great again.

'Everyone of us on the board realises the wonderful job of work that Willie Waddell is doing for the club. It is an education to work alongside him.'

Needless to say that while Hope like the other directors, is ready to back Waddell and encourage him, too, if that is necessary, he would never interfere. He says: 'Willie Waddell is the man for the job. It is as simple as that. We do not believe that there could be anyone else doing the job for Rangers.'

And so, the job that Hope does for the Club is on the financial side where he has proved such a wizard with figures. It was only last season that Sir Isaac Wolfson visited Ibrox and left impressed by Hope's business acumen.

Yet, there was a time when he was used as a scout for Rangers and I was with him on his mission to Norway to watch an international centre-forward who had been recommended to the club. We travelled to Oslo one June several years back to see Norway face Bulgaria in an international match at the Ulleval Stadium. The man Hope had been asked to watch by Manager Scot Symon was Odd Iveson of the First Division club Rosenborg.

I still remember as I watched that game wondering how Hope would react to the obvious rawness of the tall centre-forward. I anticipated that like most directors he would happily pass the buck, head back for Scotland suggesting that someone else should take another look at the player.

I was wrong. Hope's knowledge of football, gained in twenty long years in the juniors, stood him in good stead that night. He told me immediately after the game as we made our way back to our hotel: 'He is not nearly ready to come to Rangers. There are too many rough edges to get rid of. We are looking for a player who can step straight into our first team pool. Iveson is not of that standard. I was ready to invite him back to Ibrox if he measured up but he doesn't and that's that.'

Hope's decision was the correct one and it underlined again

the single-mindedness of the man. That same single-mindedness which has brought the gold of the pools flowing unceasingly into Ibrox. Which has brought the luxury of the social club to the Rangers' fans and their families. Which will bring a super stadium for the same fans very soon.

Says Hope: 'All of the improvements that have been made already and will be made in the future will be paid for out of the pool funds. This is what the pool is for, to increase the amenities for the fans.

'And, after all, we have to make these improvements because they are part of the changing face of football. It is no longer enough for a man to stroll along on a Saturday afternoon, pay his money and stand on the bare terracings in all kinds of weather. We have cover at Ibrox now for close on sixty thousand fans and the next aspect we will be examining is the increase in the number of seats available. This will also have to be done.

'The fans today want a bit of comfort. They can have that in the social club where they are now able to have a drink or a meal before or after the game and they will get it once work begins on the new Ibrox. More and more women are going to games with their husbands or boy friends . . . we want to have facilities that will keep them coming!'

Eventually, though the plans are still secret, what Hope and the rest of the Rangers' officials must visualise at Ibrox is a stadium where there is cover for everyone and seats for most. If this is Hope's dream then look for it coming true possibly around the time of Rangers' centenary celebrations in 1973. It must come true because all of Hope's dreams up to now have done so.

The social club has been completed. That dream has survived a fire to bring some luxury into the life of the supporters. Now there are moves to carry them beyond their 'blue heaven', moves that will stem from the seemingly endless flow of money from the pools scheme which was Hope's brain-child. When the Rangers' Chairman John Lawrence publicly praises the industry and imagination of David Hope he does not exaggerate. For Hope has laid the off-field foundation for the Rangers of the future.

Rangers' centre forward Colin Stein gets in a shot at goal in the first
Cup Final Clash as Celtic's George Connelly moves in too late with his
tackle.

The League and Cup Contrast

THE startling contrast between the heroics that Rangers performed in the Scottish Cup and the dismal displays they so often turned in during the League Championship was the season's greatest mystery for the loyal Ibrox fans.

On the one hand they had a team who had given up any hopes of even challenging for the Scottish First Division title before Christmas. And, on the other, a team that brought style and flair and a hunger for success to almost all of their Cup ties.

Rangers, last season, became a team of two faces and the fans warmed to that second face, the one that the players seemed to reserve solely for the sparkling Cup performances as the season wore on. It was strange to watch as Rangers began to struggle in the League very early on, even after they had won their League Cup section and were heading for glory in that tournament. They seemed unable to string together a series of results which would keep them in contention for the title. . . .

Bravely Manager Willie Waddell kept insisting in the early part of the season that his team would still challenge strongly for the championship even as the gap between Aberdeen and Celtic and Rangers grew steadily wider. Gradually, like all of us, he realised, though, that any chance of further honours for his team, any chance of a second trophy to join the League Cup in the Ibrox trophy room, must come with the Scottish Cup.

Eventually, too, he admitted as much when he said: 'To win a League title the demands made on the players are great and any team making a championship their aim must achieve a high level of consistency. We have young players at Ibrox, many of them relatively inexperienced, and so because of that this consistency is harder to come by. Consistency comes with experience and that will come to our players in time. . . .

'Younger players relish the sudden death of a Cup competition much more than the long, hard, haul they have to face in the League.'

Ultimately, of course, the players began to think of themselves as a Cup team, and the belief grew among the fans too. The Rangers' team went through the motions, but did little more, in many of their League games and the gap between them and the leaders continued to widen. But it was so different when the Scottish Cup games came round. It was then that the fans rolled up, giving huge attendances, and knowing that they would get full value for money as their team played with flair and determination and an ambition that seemed to grow from one round to the next.

I suppose, looking back now, the first hints of failure as far as the title race was concerned had come as early as October. By that time Rangers had drawn 0–0 with St. Mirren at Love Street when the Paisley men had defended stubbornly in the opening League game of the season; had lost 2–0 to Celtic at Celtic Park; and had crashed 2–0 on their own ground to League-leading Aberdeen. That gap had started to open even then. . . .

Then, the following month their League hopes were finished inside four tragic days when they slumped to two more defeats away from home. At the time Manager Willie Waddell, quite naturally, would not accept that the League hopes had disappeared. That is not Rangers' way . . . but most people realised with these defeats that any challenge the Ibrox men might have mounted was over.

On November 21 I was at Somerset Park in Ayr when Ally McLeod's part-time Ayr United team set about the mighty Rangers and beat them 2–1. It was a notable victory for the little Ayrshire team. Iain Whitehead and Quinton Young scored their goals and bottles of champagne were opened in the Ayr dressing room as the celebrations began at the end of the match.

Really, poor Rangers were criticised a little too harshly by their angry fans for that particular result. It was not as big a disgrace as some of the supporters seemed to think. Ayr had played well and they deserved to win . . . just as much as they did not deserve to lose a few weeks later when Celtic paid

Top left: Reserve team right back Tom Alexander, another player who broke through to the first team

Top right: George Donaldson, the fifteen year old mid-field player who was chosen to tour West Germany by Manager Willie Waddell before the season began

Bottom left: Striker Derek Parlane, one of Anderson's tips for the top among his reserve players

Bottom right: Ian MacDonald, the young left winger at Ibrox who is rated as the best opponent Jardine has had to face since his move to right back

their visit to Somerset Park. The other half of the Old Firm won 2–1 that day. A reverse of the Rangers' result, but afterwards Celtic players and officials admitted it was one of their hardest games of the season, and that Ayr had deserved at least a point for their efforts. It was a sobering thought that Scotland's two most powerful clubs should have been treated with such little regard by the part-timers of Ayr. But the Somerset Park boss Ally McLeod pointed out: 'My players rise to the challenge when we have to face up to the Old Firm. When they come down to Somerset then our lads play a little bit harder and the Celtic and Rangers' players know they'll get it tough. Let's face it, we beat Rangers and we should have beaten Celtic. They were the luckiest team in Scotland to get away from our ground without losing. We don't believe in letting the Old Firm have things all their own way. . . .'

That's the way it was when Rangers lost and then four days later came that second defeat when the Ibrox men had travelled to Easter Road, Edinburgh, to face Hibs in a postponed League match. This time, Rangers deserved to win. They outplayed Hibs for most of the game, were leading 2–1 with the match almost over and then lost two late goals, and the game, and

This is a series of six photographs taken at the Scottish Cup Final replay. They show teenage centre forward Derek Johnstone as he forces the Celtic defence into the mistake that brought Rangers their only goal of the game. It was an own goal by the Celtic right back Jim Craig.

1. Johnstone's shot for goal strikes goalkeeper Evan Williams' foot as Jim Craig and Tom Callaghan, partially hidden by the young Ranger, watch anxiously.

their last chance of staying close to the League leaders. It was an unbelievable lapse by Rangers. If you won't take my word for it then you might accept the verdict of Liverpool's manager, Bill Shankly.

I can still remember being with Shankly a few days after that game down at his own ground Anfield. He had motored north for the Easter Road game to conduct a spying mission on Hibs, his club's opponents in the Fairs Cup, and had left before the match was over. Left, in fact, when Rangers were leading 2-1 and coasting to the two points they wanted.

Said Shankly: 'We were on our way back home to Liverpool in the car when the final result of the match came over on the car radio. I couldn't believe it. I was convinced that there must have been some kind of mistake because Rangers had been so much in command of the situation when I left. I couldn't see any way for Hibs to win . . . and I didn't believe it until I heard the score for the second time on a later news bulletin!'

But while it tested Bill Shankly's credulity that just happened to be the way that Rangers were when it came to League games. The consistency, even the concentration, that was necessary wasn't there. It hadn't been achieved by the younger players and so the League was decided without a real contribution being made by Rangers. They had no say in the final destination of the League flag.

2. The panic is on in the Celtic defence as Johnstone wheels away from the action. The ball is seen here breaking from between Williams and Callaghan and running towards Craig.

3. The moment as Craig tries to clear the ball from the line as Callaghan and Williams await the outcome.

5. Disbelief turns to despair as the Celtic players realise what has happened and a jubilant Ranger, left back Willie Mathieson races into the picture.

4. It's total disbelief among the Celtic defenders as the ball screws from Craig's foot and spins over the line and into the net to give Rangers a goal.

6. Disgust from Craig, anger from goalkeeper Williams, anguish from Callaghan . . . but unrestrained joy from Willie Mathieson. All the emotions of a moment of drama from the Cup Final replay are caught here.

If anyone was left, of course, who still believed that there was a challenge after the defeats at Ayr and Easter Road then in December two more blows fell. First of all Dundee arrived at Ibrox, retreated into defence to steal a 0–0 draw at the start of December. Then, a week later, Rangers travelled to Perth to face St. Johnstone, transformed into a highly attractive, goal getting combination by their manager Willie Ormond. Again there was defeat . . . this time by 2–1 and now even at Ibrox they admitted that their title ambitions had withered and died.

Again Rangers were criticised for this result. Again there were people among the fans who refused to acknowledge that teams such as Ayr United and St. Johnstone had been able to prove their ability against other teams. Quite simply, it is no disgrace these days to lose to St. Johnstone at Muirton Park. Once it was an easy matter to collect two points at Perth . . . not so very long ago, either! A jaunt up to Perth was a pleasant day out for the big teams from Glasgow. An easy match in the quiet country town where the pitch was placed in an ideal setting with the Perthshire hills providing a peaceful back-drop to the game when you watch it from the stand. There was little to worry the big guns . . . all they had to do was pick up the two points by the end of the game.

But, now, the ex-Hibs' winger Willie Ormond has changed all that. He has developed a team with a sound, steady, if unspectacular defence and a forward line with two outstanding individualists in John Connolly and Henry Hall. Once more St. Johnstone weren't happy to rest on their laurels after beating Rangers. They did the Muirton double over the Old Firm by beating Celtic 3–2 and at the end of the season had risen to third place in the League, just ahead of Rangers.

Right after that Muirton match Rangers headed for West Germany and the preparation for the Scottish Cup campaign which was to start in January. The opener for the Cup, the first round game at the end of January, was against Falkirk. There was no easy run in for the Ibrox men. In a way they were starting in the Scottish Cup the way they had in the Fairs Cup when they had drawn Bayern Munich. The chance to play themselves in had been denied them in the European competition . . . now at home the same had happened. Falkirk were one of the newly-promoted teams but in only half a season they had confirmed themselves as formidable opposition to any of the First Division teams who had met them.

26   They had forced themselves into a position close to the top

of the table at the time of the Cup clash, being handled shrewdly by the former Northern Ireland World Cup player and ex-Dunfermline manager Willie Cunningham. Admittedly they had been tagged a defensive team and their main aim in so many of their matches away from home had been to contain the opposition attacks, rather than try to set up their own moves. It was building into a cracking tie before the kick-off with Falkirk predicting how they would knock Rangers out of the Cup and the Ibrox men preparing calmly but possibly a little bit apprehensively for the first Scottish tie of the year.

Falkirk, though, were not given the slightest chance to drop into their defensive shell which had by this time become notorious in Scotland. Rangers went out to hit them and hit them hard and with Willie Johnston in the mood the Falkirk defence was destroyed. The jet-paced Johnston snapped two goals himself and young Alfie Conn grabbed another for Rangers to reach the next round on an easy 3–0 score line which immediately raised the Cup hopes of the 41,000 fans who were at Ibrox that afternoon.

The next game brought a chance for revenge against one of the teams who had cost Rangers points in the League. They were drawn against another First Division team, St. Mirren, at Paisley, where they had dropped a point in the very first League match of the season. There was never the slightest danger of a repeat of the ignominious showing which had earned Rangers only a goalless draw that first time round. Any challenge Saints were ready to put up was brushed aside as Rangers powered their way to the Cup form that was beginning to follow them and went on to win 3–1. It was another excellent performance and another to cheer the 36,000 fans who were at Love Street, many of whom had been suffering the dreary displays in the League.

Then followed the greatest revenge of all for Rangers and their legions of supporters. For in the third round they were paired with the holders of the trophy, Aberdeen, the team who were leading the League and looking like powerful pretenders to Celtic's title. Under Manager Eddie Turnbull the men from Pittodrie had been leading the race for the championship almost since the season opened. On their way to that proud number one spot, too, they had come to Ibrox and beaten Rangers 2–0. Hence, the revenge tag that hung around the match.

In a League game in Aberdeen just two weeks before the   27

More drama and a near escape for Bayern Munich in the Ibrox Fairs
Cup tie. The ball is cleared here by Bayern defender George
Schwarzenbeck as goalkeeper Sepp Maier goes down in a heap with
Rangers' Colin Jackson.

Cup clash the two teams had drawn o–o in a fiercely fought battle. Now the decider had come. This was the sudden-death game, the crunch . . . and Rangers were the team to survive it. Ironically for Aberdeen, the goal, the solitary goal that was needed to decide the tie came from the only Aberdonian on the Rangers' playing staff, sweeper Colin Jackson. The tall defender had taken to coming upfield for corners and free kicks during the season, *a la* Jackie Charlton. He had occasionally been successful, but never before as successful as he was that day. His goal took Rangers into the semi-finals at a time when once again most people were a little too ready to predict a defeat for the Ibrox men. In this game Rangers dictated the way things were going to go from the start. They were in command, just another example of the poise that followed them in the Cup.

When they were paired with Hibs in the semi-final the draw meant that Rangers had had by far the hardest road of any team left in the Cup. Every match they had played had been against First Division opposition. And, in every match, there had been doubts expressed as to whether or not they would survive because of their lack-lustre League performances.

The fans had been converted, though, by the Cup displays. These had convinced the vast majority of the Rangers' supporters that this was, indeed, their Cup year and that the Scottish Cup would soon be with the League Cup.

The first semi-final game against Hibs brought them back to earth a little. The Easter Road team were quite unmindful of the fact that this was a match of some standing in Scottish soccer. So, they came to Hampden to defend, they faced Rangers in a sudden death Cup game with only one idea . . . to stop Rangers playing. They succeeded to a great extent to do just that. They held back in defence using only two attackers upfield for most of the game and, in the end, they achieved a goalless draw which pleased no one in the 69,000 crowd which had come to Hampden.

Yet, in spite of the drab tactics of Hibs and the lack of goals, this became a game which stirred up passions off the field. For, Hibs' boss Dave Ewing launched an attack on Rangers after the game using the now notorious remark: 'Rangers are rubbish. . . .'

When that comment from Ewing hit the headlines the next morning Rangers and their fans were furious. I can still remember Manager Willie Waddell telling me in his Ibrox office: 'It is a different matter for the Rangers' fans to criticise the club if they have played badly, than it is for a rival manager to talk in this way. This comment will unite the Rangers' support behind the team for the replay. I am convinced of that.

'I don't particularly want to get involved in a slanging match with Hibs but I would have thought that Mr. Ewing had enough problems of his own to handle without concerning himself about the problems of the Rangers Football Club.'

Waddell was right, of course, the fans did rally round the team, Ewing was jeered at the replay, and the Rangers' players showed their own displeasure by getting goals from Willie Henderson and Alfie Conn to reach the final on a 2–1 victory. The rest of the League games were played out in the same manner as the others, bursts of good form, as when they beat Kilmarnock 4–1 at Rugby Park in their last game, and lapses, like when they lost to St. Johnstone at Ibrox. That cost Rangers third place in the League to the Perth team and also gave Saints their first-ever League double over the Ibrox club. Then it was onto the final, and the replay, both of which have been covered by skipper John Greig in another chapter.

In this coming season I am certain that the consistency which was missing last year will be demanded from the players. They have matured a little, are older and more experienced and they now know, all of them, what exactly is expected of Rangers' players. Somehow I don't anticipate the League race being deserted quite so quickly or so happily as it was last year.

Ibrox Manager Willie Waddell has always maintained: 'The real test for any team is to win the League title. Teams can win Cups and can be good teams doing it but the long haul to a League title requires a consistency of performance that only the best teams can produce. A League title is the prize in football that is the most difficult of all to win. It is the prize that I want for Rangers. . . .'

The moment that Rangers and their fans had waited for . . . the
moment that an Ibrox skipper held aloft a major trophy once
again. The man with the Leaue Cup is centre-half Ronnie
McKinnon who captained the team against Celtic in the final of the
tournament at Hampden

The League Cup
Returns to Ibrox

IT WAS building up to be one of the most one-sided League
Cup Finals in the history of the tournament . . . the bookies
made Celtic odds-on favourites, an unheard of event in any
Old Firm clash . . . Scotland's soccer stars went almost 100 per
cent for a Celtic victory . . . it seemed that Rangers were going
to Hampden simply to provide opposition because the occasion
demanded that of them.

As the days before the final dragged on, the feelings that this
was once again going to turn into a Celtic success story grew
stronger. At Ibrox, Rangers' Manager, Willie Waddell, and his
right-hand man, coach Jock Wallace, put the players through
their preparations with the minimum of fuss. The first team pool
were taken at the start of the week preceding the Final to the
sands at Gullane near Edinburgh where the torture training
course up and down the giant sand dunes which was set for the
team by Wallace, had become a Glasgow joke. But Waddell
and Wallace knew what they were doing. They intended to
make sure that the only thing their players had on their minds
was the coming match . . . and the peak of fitness that they
must reach before going out onto the Hampden pitch to face
Celtic.

For four and a half long years Rangers had failed to lift one
solitary soccer trophy. And in those years the club and their
fans had been taunted more and more by the sight of their
arch rivals, Celtic, carrying off so many of the Cups that they
themselves had aimed for.

The whole of Scotland, outside of the marble halls of Ibrox,
believed that the same old story was going to be repeated.

In a poll conducted by my own newspaper, the *Daily Record*,
among the other First Division skippers on the eve of the game,
the vote was overwhelmingly in favour of Celtic. The few who
did choose Rangers to win the trophy did so only because they
felt that some time, by the law of averages, the cruel run which
had denied Rangers success must change direction.

33

And so that was the background as the fans massed towards Hampden for that Old Firm confrontation on 24 October. Already that year Celtic had beaten Rangers in a Glasgow Cup Final and again in a League game at Celtic Park. The gloss of Rangers' fine quarter-final win over Hibs had been forgotten . . . and it was forgotten even more as the fans began to crowd around the great Glasgow ground.

For right before the game the odds seemed to shift even more in the direction of Celtic who were chasing their sixth successive League Cup win. There are always rumours flying around at Hampden before a big game. It is part of the scene. Only, this time, the rumours had truth to back them. This time there was substance to the interminable stories of injury and illness that surround teams on soccer's gala occasions. And the news that filtered out of the Hampden dressing-rooms and spread like wildfire around the stadium was that Rangers' skipper, John Greig, the Ibrox Iron Man for so long, had been ruled out of the game after a fitness test.

After Derek Johnstone (No.9) had scored the one and only goal against Celtic in the Scottish League Cup he turns, raises his arms and runs up the field. His team mate Conn (right of picture) runs over to congratulate him

Among Rangers' fans the news added to the gloom that was already pushing its way into their mood before the kick-off . . .

Among Celtic fans it was hailed as the final confirmation that their team was set for a Hampden walk-over.

The Greig blow had been the best-kept secret at Ibrox during the last days of training. He had gone down with 'flu in mid-week and missed the final, vitally important, days of training. Rangers had still hoped he would be able to play, but at Ibrox an hour before the Hampden kick-off, Greig decided that he was not 100 per cent fit. It was an honest decision and a courageous one. Some players might have gone out and then let the team down because they were still off colour . . . Greig is not that kind of man.

Earlier, Willie Waddell had committed himself to a team gamble, one that looked very formidable when assessed alongside the news of Greig's late withdrawal. On the Friday morning he had made up his mind to play sixteen-years-old Derek John-

The goal that decided the League Cup Final has been scored and the joy of these Rangers' players isn't hidden in this celebration picture from Hampden. The Ibrox men are left to right, Alec Miller, Colin Stein, Alex MacDonald, Willie Henderson and, congratulating scorer Derek Johnstone, Colin Jackson and Sandy Jardine. The unhappy Celt on the extreme right is Jimmy Quinn

stone as his main striker. In his début game for Rangers against Cowdenbeath he had scored twice. Now Waddell wanted him to play again and display his very special talents for scoring goals, against Celtic. He felt the move could pay off, that it could carry the League Cup back to the Ibrox trophy room.

It was another piece of news jealously guarded by the Ibrox staff until the team was announced.

Waddell had called Johnstone aside from his team-mates after the Friday morning training session, told him he would be playing before he travelled back to his home in Dundee that afternoon, and added a stern warning that the news *must not* leak out. It wasn't known until kick-off time . . .

When it hit the fans it was a shock to add to the news that Greig was out . . . yet eventually that selection by Waddell won the game for Rangers. For Derek Johnstone scored a headed goal in forty minutes of the game and wrote a page for himself in Ibrox soccer history that seemed more suitable for a schoolboy soccer serial! He was three weeks short of his seventeenth birthday . . . the youngest player in Britain ever to play—never mind score—in a match of this importance . . . and suddenly he was elevated to the ranks of greats scattered through the history of the Ibrox club. For Johnstone's goal wasn't simply the goal that beat Celtic, nor even the goal that won the League Cup . . . it was the goal which ended the trophy famine at Ibrox. The goal which brought them a Cup after the longest run of non-success in their proud history.

To Rangers' fans, too, it meant the possibility of a new era for their club, the team they had stuck by so loyally in the lean years. Now success had returned less than a year after Willie Waddell was installed in the manager's chair.

Waddell had made changes in the team. He had concentrated on young players, fresh players, players from Rangers' own nursery of starlets, and he had succeeded in building a team to win a trophy. That night, as he left Hampden, Waddell told me: 'We didn't look on ourselves as underdogs in the game. People could say what they liked, it didn't worry us one bit. I've been thirty years in football and I have yet to go into any game feeling the slightest bit inferior to the opposition.

'I really can't praise the young players too highly for the job they have done for me and for the club. They have all worked so very hard this season. They have had to do a lot which was hard on them but not once have I heard a complaint from any of them. That in itself says a lot for their character.'

Then he added: 'This victory can be an inspiration to the young players and a filip to the more established players, as well. They have been needing this breakthrough.

'And that's how we look on this . . . as a breakthrough. What we must do now is to consolidate on this win, to keep going after other trophies. This has to be the start of something for this team. It is a beginning, a starting point, and more must follow before I am satisfied.'

Later Waddell admitted to me that he had not anticipated the breakthrough to come so soon. He had gone overboard for a youth policy. He had lost experienced stars and had turned

A duel between midfield men, Alex MacDonald of Rangers (left) and Bobby Murdoch Celtic (right), in the League Cup Final at Hampden. Celt Harry Hood waits to see the outcome

to players who had not been established first-team men when he arrived at Ibrox.

In the team that found success that day at Hampden, he had Sandy Jardine and Alec Miller at full-back, Colin Jackson had slotted solidly into the heart of the defence alongside Ronnie

Another near thing for Celtic as goal-keeper Evan Williams smothers the ball on the line as Rangers' striker Colin Stein races in to challenge. Goal-scorer Derek Johnstone appeals to the referee that the ball has crossed the line while the two Celts in the background, No. 6, David Hay and Jimmy Quinn appeal that no goal has been scored. The Celts were right this time . . .

McKinnon, Alfie Conn showed a mid-field mastery that he had always promised but never really fulfilled until that famous match, and Derek Johnstone had, of course, scored the goal None of these players had been first-team men when Waddell was appointed Rangers' saviour. Yet suddenly on that October

afternoon they had become the men who led **Rangers** out of the darkness.

I will never forget John Greig after that match. He must have been bitterly disappointed. He had been forced out of the game by illness and suffered agonies as he sat on the bench willing the youngsters he had helped and encouraged so often, towards victory against Rangers' oldest and most deadly rivals. In four and a half long years he had skippered Rangers magnificently and now in their moment of glory he had not been playing. Yet Greig shrugged aside his own personal disappointment and burst on to the field to be first to congratulate his team-mates. And after the game, outside the victory dressing-room, he told me: 'They were great, weren't they? Half of these players are only boys in the game and yet they played fantastic football out there.

'You know, some of us were starting to think we were jinxed when it came to winning trophies, especially against the Celtic. We seemed to get so close and then it would all crumble away. Now I think that these days are over as far as we are concerned.

'The funny thing about it all is that so many of the **lads** who played today are winning their first honour. That must be a boost to them. It's an unusual situation for Rangers' players to be in.

'When I was a younger player, winning medals was almost a habit. Willie Henderson and Ron McKinnon are the same . . . we know what it is like to win Cups and Leagues. The young players didn't know until this afternoon and it must have opened up a whole new world for them.'

Of course, one victory didn't suddenly sweep away all the problems that Waddell faced in building the kind of team he wanted. There were times in the League campaign when a strange inconsistency struck at the players, when results went against the team, when the supporters tasted disappointment once again. But consistency is not a quality which is easily come by, particularly by young and relatively inexperienced players.

Waddell accepted that—perhaps not always happily—but he did accept it. He maintained that consistency would only come with experience and that this Rangers' team would be a better Cup team than a League championship challenging team, that the knock-out atmosphere of the Cup was better suited to their attitude. And so the major target after the League Cup became the Scottish Cup.

The League, the prize that Waddell wants most of all, had to wait until the team had matured.

Celtic's centre-half Billy McNeill (No. 5) looks on as Colin Stein,
Rangers falls over Celtic's goal-keeper Williams—Jackson
(Rangers) waits for the ball to drop

It's that man McKinnon in the thick of things again as he rises in a heading duel with Aberdeen's powerful striker Dave Robb. Also in the picture is Henderson, (left) and Smith (right), of Rangers

The Feud that Back-fired

I'M NOT USUALLY the type of player who becomes involved in feuds with opponents. I'll go out of my way to avoid trouble either on or off the park . . . but last season I found it hard to stick by that. In fact, I found it almost impossible not to become involved in an off-field slanging match with West Germany's international centre-forward, Gerd Muller.

For Herr Muller proved to me and to the rest of my Rangers' team-mates that his talent for scoring goals was only equalled by his talent for stirring up trouble away from the actual games. I became his target for this kind of campaign, but now, looking back at the trouble-making he got up to I reckon that the feud he tried to get going with me back-fired on him.

Anyhow, the background to the whole affair is that Rangers and Muller's club team, Bayern Munich, were drawn against each other in the first round of the European Fairs Cup at the start of last season. It was a major tie for both teams and the outstanding game of that first-round draw. It came immediately on top of West German's great World Cup run in Mexico and their eventual third placing there. And, in the Bayern team were three of their World Cup heroes, goalkeeper Sepp Maier, and the two biggest stars in German soccer, sweeper Franz Beckenbauer and the ace goal snatcher, Muller.

Now, we knew about them besides their exploits in Mexico, mainly because Scotland had played against West Germany in two World Cup qualifying games.

I had played in both these games, and, of course, several other Rangers' players had been involved as well. Going further back, we had met Bayern in the final of the European Cup Winners Cup in 1967 in Nuremberg, when we had lost by the only goal of the game in extra time. In all three of these games I had been directly opposed to Muller and I had gained a great admiration for his ability to find space—and dangerous positions—in the penalty box. I had a great respect for him and, at the same time, I had always found him friendly enough off the field when the

43

games were finished. Along with Beckenbauer, I had always felt that Muller was the kind of player you could mix easily with at any receptions or banquets that follow big games.

How wrong can you get?

The days before we were scheduled to fly out to Munich for the first-leg game against the West German club, the muck raking, mud slinging and general trouble-making moves began with an article by Muller in a national Sunday newspaper. He not only criticised me . . . but he tried his best to get more trouble going by drawing on the old rivalry between Rangers and Celtic to needle me further. In that article Muller wrote: 'Every time I play against Ronnie McKinnon I strike top form. Celtic's Billy McNeill is a world-class centre-half, but McKinnon is not and I cannot understand why Scotland pick McKinnon before the Celtic man. . . .'

When I heard about the attack first of all I was furious. I don't think I've ever been so angry because I couldn't see that I had done anything to Muller to deserve such a blast off from him.

Then, when I sat down to think about it, I gradually saw what Muller was up to. He was setting out to deliberately get me angry. He wanted me to be so annoyed with him when the game came along that I would allow my concentration to be affected. When that dawned on me I made up my mind that I would never allow that to happen. I felt it was essential for me to concentrate only on the game, to forget Muller and all his big talk and his insults, and simply go out to play so well that he would be forced to eat his words. I doubt if I have ever gone into any game with such determination to do well as I did that night in the Bayern stadium in Munich. I suppose, in a way, I was still annoyed, but it was a controlled anger. And I knew it had to stay that way. . . .

I felt then, and I still feel the same today, that it is bad sportsmanship to run down a fellow professional in the manner used by Muller. It isn't the kind of thing that I would like to indulge in . . . even if I did feel, as Muller might have done, that it would give me an edge over my opponent when it came to playing the game. I believe that games are won out on the field, not by shouting your mouth off either before or afterwards.

I suppose I felt a bit let down at the time because I had thought that Muller and I had a mutual respect built up for each other after the games we had played in opposition. It had seemed to me that we'd finished about even in these games.

This time, though, I was determined to get on top of him. I had always felt that his main danger lay in the penalty area. When he drifts deep or goes out to the wings then he isn't the most difficult centre-forward in the world to deal with.

It isn't in any of these positions on the park that he does his damage. He is the type of centre-forward who does all his dangerous work, all his destruction of defences, right there in the vital area of the penalty box. It is inside the 18 yards' line that you must watch him like a hawk because he has a shrewd positional sense and an unrivalled ability for snatching the scantest of chances. In an earlier edition of this Rangers' book I summed him up this way: 'He (Muller) thinks only of scoring goals. He isn't so good in the air, he isn't terribly fast, he hasn't got a tremendously strong shot . . . but give him the slightest glimpse of goal and he will score for you. He is the master of the half chance. . . .' I haven't changed my mind any on that assessment. But the professional friendship that I felt I might have with Muller off the field has soured as far as I am concerned. I didn't talk to him at all after the first game in Munich, and at Ibrox where the tie was settled I simply shook hands and left it at that.

In that first-leg game in Munich we were desperately unlucky to lose to the West Germans. We went there and opened out at them a little bit more than we might normally have done in a European tie away from home, and it came close to paying off for us. You see, we caught them by surprise. I honestly believe that the Bayern coach, Udo Lattek, had underestimated us. They didn't anticipate that we would hit them the way that we did. Sure, we lost the game 1–0, to a goal from Franz Beckenbauer, but John Greig hit the bar and in the end we finished up with more scoring chances than they managed in front of their own fans. Our coach, Jock Wallace, had been to see Bayern on one of these invaluable spy missions that clubs set up before an important game on the Continent.

These trips have become tremendously important in the pre-match preparations of any team involved in European competitions. It used to be that on many occasions we went into a game in Europe blind, not really knowing what to expect. Perhaps, if we were lucky, we knew some of the opposing players from playing against them in internationals, or else from their reputations. Mostly, though, we knew next to nothing about the opposing team's tactics or playing pattern. Anyhow, that was in the early days. Now things have changed and Jock Wallace was able to tell us what we had to watch for when we came up against Bayern. We knew that the elegant Beckenbauer still played deep, lying behind the back four defenders for his club, breaking out only occasionally to move upfield. We contained him for most of the game, keeping him occupied at the back except for the one move

45

Two photographs taken in sequence when John Greig broke through the German defence as (left to right) Beckenbauer, Mrosko and Schwarzenbeck come into tackle. The picture is a pat on the head from German keeper Maier. John Greig, breaks through the Bayern defence and gets a shot at goal

Beckenbauer (left) walks up field as his keeper Maier taps John Greig on the head after an effort from him had gone over the bar

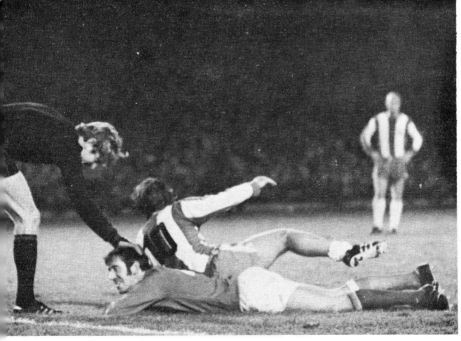

This is the kind of determination that Ronnie McKinnon showed
against Gerd Muller in the two games against Bayern Munich.
Here he clears from Hibs' forward Kenny Davidson as Joe Baker
watches anxiously

when he appeared in our half and scored with a bit of a lucky shot from something like 35 yards away from our goal. Other than that he was forced to stay back much more than he would normally have done in a game at his own ground in front of his own fans. That swung the game our way a little, I suppose, because Beckenbauer is the truly great creative player in their team.

Muller, I'm happy to say, had a quiet time despite the boasts of what he might do when he came up against me again. We were all delighted that we had gone back to Glasgow just one goal behind. We knew that two goals were enough to give us victory and a place in the next round. And, we knew, too, that the Germans had been frightened by the way we had played.

In particular, they were frightened of our outside-left, Willie Johnston. When they arrived in Glasgow for the second-leg game at Ibrox, the Bayern coach, Lattek, told the whole of Scotland: 'Johnston is the player we fear'. The reason for that was that Willie had had the best game I've ever seen him play in that first-leg game. He had jetted clear of their full-back time and again, and most of our danger had started from him.

The worry for us as we prepared for the match became the problem of how we would cope if Willie was marked out of the game—as seemed likely from the Bayern pronouncements. Well, as it happened, Bayern played their Danish international star, Jonny Hansen, at right-back with obvious instructions to shadow Willie out of the game. He played so tightly on Willie that he was kept quiet for most of the match. That tactic was part of their general defensive plan. Beckenbauer proved himself once again the most stylish sweeper in the world and the key man in their defensive set up. They held out well and the game ended in a 1–1 draw which meant we were out of the Fairs Cup after holding such high hopes of doing well in the tournament. Unhappily for me, Gerd Muller did score this time, with a free kick from not too far outside the penalty box which hit off the inside of the post and finished up in the net. I wasn't pleased that he had scored, even though I felt in my own mind that over the two games I had managed to prove to him and to anyone else who agreed with him that I wasn't the easy mark he made out!

We had been desperately unlucky over the two games. Unlucky in Munich where we had outplayed Bayern for long spells. Unlucky at Ibrox where we had had almost all the game but just couldn't get the goals we needed, and that meant defeat. But despite the defeat, despite being out of Europe so early, our manager, Willie Waddell, gave us a special bonus for our performance. After the League game the following Saturday he took all of the members of the first team pool to the luxury Turnberry Hotel on the Ayrshire coast for a few days' golfing holiday. That proved to us that we had done all we could have done in our attempt to win the tie. The Boss is a hard taskmaster. He doesn't give away treats like holidays to the players unless we have earned them. It's not his way. So, when we were told that we were being taken to Turnberry that week we knew that in his book we had been a success against Bayern in the two tough games.

It was disappointing, but the quality of Bayern as a team was underlined in the very next round when they took on Coventry City from the English First Division and hammered six goals past them in the first-leg game in Munich. When I think of how close we were to *winning* in Munich, and then consider the Coventry score, then I doubt if I need to emphasise just how well we had played in that first round Fairs Cup tie.

The biggest let down from that result was, of course, being out of competitive European football for the next year. Playing in top games against top teams from the Continent is an important way for any player to further his soccer education. And, what's more, these glamour games provide any clubs' fans with a bonus during the season.

The ironic thing about the first round knock out was that on the form we had displayed over the two games we would have been able to beat so many of the teams in the tournament. It was just our luck last season to meet up with Bayern and then, when we did, fail to get the breaks that our play should have earned us.

Still, there will be other years and some of these seasons Rangers will win a European trophy. I'm convinced of that. We prepare so thoroughly for these games and gradually the younger players are gaining the experience needed to adapt to these Continental clashes. The matches abroad that the Boss arranged for us later in the season were tremendous for the players who don't have so very much experience behind them for European games.

Anyhow, personally, all I want is to have another crack at Bayern Munich and Gerd Muller. I would like to meet up with them some time in the future and to finish up on the winning side against them. For Rangers I have faced them three times, lost twice by a single goal, on each occasion in West Germany, and drawn at Ibrox. For Scotland I have faced Muller twice, again losing by a single goal in West Germany and drawing at Hampden. To beat either his club or his international team when I am directly opposed to Muller would give me great delight.

For one thing it might help shut him up a little bit more. I think that in those games against Bayern I made my points on the field. 'Der Bomber' as he is known in West Germany—was remarkably quiet after his pre-match burst of propaganda . . . but a defeat would possibly silence him forever as far as the off-field insults go.

I like to think that my chance might come to do that. Anyhow, after the games last year I think that he possibly realises now that he might have been better to keep quiet. His feud was a flop. I didn't allow my anger to affect my concentration the way he wanted. I simply made up my mind that in that penalty area I would stick closer to him than I had ever stuck to any other player in my whole career. . . .

That's why I still believe today that Muller's feud back-fired. If he had said nothing then maybe I would not have been so determined to stop him. Instead of gaining an advantage as he had hoped, Muller's mouth just made things hard for himself.

It's Ronnie McKinnon to the rescue as he clears off the line with Celtic inside-right Harry Hood running in

West Germany—Rangers Training Ground for Europe

THE ever-recurring theme of Rangers' Manager Willie Waddell during his first full season as the Ibrox supremo was one of youth.

Waddell had made up his mind the previous season to concentrate on a youth policy. And when the time came for preparations to be made for his first full year in control he began them by dropping a tour party bombshell. For when he named his party of players to visit West Germany prior to the start of the Scottish season he included 15-year-old Edinburgh boy George Donaldson as one of his mid-field men.

The news was released from Ibrox at the time of the Commonwealth Games in Edinburgh, at a time when the whole of Scotland was being thrilled by the performances of young athletes and swimmers in the games at the Meadowbank Stadium. And, on the day Waddell decided on his pool of players for the two-game trip he told me determinedly: 'I have been impressed by young George in training and in the practice games we have held so far. But what has helped me make up my mind about this is the things I have been watching at the Commonwealth Games. I have been sitting at home and watching the television and seeing youngsters of thirteen, *thirteen*, winning medals in the swimming events. If they can do that then there is no need for me to worry overmuch about a lad of 15. I'm convinced that he will be able to do a job for me on the football field. If I didn't think so then he wouldn't be going. Age shouldn't be too much of a barrier in these days.'

Waddell had chosen West Germany as the starting point for his new super-fit Rangers and it wasn't too difficult to understand why he had done so.

I had been with the Rangers' boss in West Germany several times as a fellow-journalist. I knew that this was a country whose football he admired as well as being a country where Rangers were well-known and respected. It was also a country where Waddell believed a team would not be able to coast along in

53

A look at Rangers' striker Colin Stein in action against Falkirk in a Cup game at Ibrox . . . but in West Germany, Stein was ordered off in the first game against Hamburg at the Volkspark Stadium. In this picture the Falkirk players are goalkeeper Stewart Rennie and captain George Miller

easy, relaxed friendlies . . . it was a country where a team would be made to play to get results!

Waddell didn't want to know about holiday trips for his players. He didn't want to know about easy warm-up games to break his team in gently for what lay ahead of them. He was plain in his views, straight-ahead with his ideas . . . he wanted tough games, testing games and West Germany was one country where he knew he would get them.

Happily, when we set off from Glasgow Airport to head for the first game in Hamburg against Uwe Seeler's team, no one in the party realised just how tough the pre-season games were going to be. It was as well that way, otherwise there might have been a few long faces instead of the smiles of anticipation at the airport that July morning.

The hand-picked opposition was predictably severe. Hamburg on their own Volkspark Stadium was a tough nut to crack at any time. The other opponents Rangers were to meet, Kaiserslautern, were not so well known, perhaps, but were still a team who had ended the previous season comfortably placed in the middle of the Bundesliga, the West German super league. Added to that, both of the West German clubs had already played friendly games. Rangers had been limited to practice games.

If that wasn't worry enough for the Ibrox men they had hit troubles of their own on the eve of departure. Goalkeeper Peter McCloy went down with a virus infection and called off and skipper John Greig damaged an ankle in a five-a-side tournament at Musselburgh. Greig was with the group which flew out of Glasgow but his ankle was swollen and painful and we knew that he would not be able to play in the Hamburg opener.

This game was generally reckoned to be the harder of the two with Hamburg ready to field two of their World Cup stars, defender Willi Schulz and centre forward Uwe Seeler. When Rangers went a goal down after just one minute of that first game I think all the Scots in the crowd—soldiers and holiday-makers—realised that this was not going to be their night. It was a goal from a free kick which had been awarded after Alex MacDonald had pulled down local hero Seeler. Zaczyk took the kick and hit it into the net from 30 yards. It was a bad goal to lose and reserve 'keeper Gerry Neef back playing in front of his own countrymen was suspect. When Honig scored a second in 38 minutes Rangers were in trouble—but the biggest sensation of the whole trip was still to come. As the players were running back into position following the goal we suddenly saw the West German referee, Uhlrich Wolf race to centre-forward

Colin Stein, speak to him and then point dramatically to the dressing-rooms. Stein was being ordered off for the sixth time in his career and this time no one in the press box knew the reason for his dismissal. It was a mystery that could only be solved by Herr Wolf. At half-time I struggled down to the dressing-rooms, set deep in the heart of the vast stadium, to be told by the referee: 'Stein was sent off for punching the Hamburg player Kurnjuhn.' It was an incident no one had seen, including Hamburg officials. But, mystery or not, it was another ordering-off on Stein's record and Rangers were left with just ten men.

In a foreign country, in front of a mainly hostile crowd, Rangers were left to fight on without their ace striker. They fought well. That was an encouragement for Manager Waddell. The ten men scored a goal through Billy Mathieson, their left-back, and although they lost another goal to Honig near the end they looked a great deal more impressive after half time. Even with ten men, even without the inspiration of skipper John Greig, even with the inexperience in the team, Rangers refused to lie down to the powerful Hamburg side.

The encouragement that Waddell drew from the performance that night came from their fighting spirit, from the fine first-team comeback after his leg break by 'sweeper' Dave Smith and from the confident goalkeeping of young Bobby Watson who had replaced Neef after ten minutes of the second half.

So, as we moved on to Kaiserslautern there was still a feeling of optimism . . . and a determination among the players to win this second game. Yet once more, Rangers hit trouble . . . a near brawl during the game and another player being ordered off! It had seemed impossible for there to be any trouble at all in that quiet little town in southern Germany. Rangers were entertained to a civic reception before the game. The club officials welcomed the Scots, the burgomaster made polite noises and the Kaiserslautern coach, Michaele Lorant, a member of the famous Hungarian team of the 50s had said how much he was looking forward to the game. On the night of the match everything seemed peaceful. The crowd were in a holiday mood. Two teams of young girls played an exhibition game before the big match, a local high school band played and any trouble seemed far away . . .

But the warmth of the welcome had not been passed on to the players. The Kaiserslautern men seemed determined that Rangers were not going to leave with a result.

In particular they had a Yugoslav inside-forward named Hosic who was bent on making trouble from the very first minutes of the game . . . and ultimately it was Hosic who was the player involved in the incident which saw the second Rangers' player being sent off in two successive matches. This time the victim was teenager Kenny Watson who had come on as a substitute in 59 minutes, tangled with Hosic twice and was then sent off nine minutes after his appearance following a third clash with the balding Slav. It was a harsh decision in that while Watson was ordered off Hosic remained on the field to cause more bother and referee Karl Ditmer took no action at all against him. Eventually Rangers went in front through a penalty goal scored by Andy Penman and then, in injury time, the Germans were awarded a penalty and equalised. It had been a rough, tough, untidy kind of game with that holiday feeling of the crowd giving way to anger before the end. It was the kind of hostile feeling that normally accompanies a competitive European game and so Willie Waddell was not too concerned about it.

He was concerned, though, with the Watson ordering-off decision. And he said so.

I can still remember him angrily telling me in Frankfurt Airport the next morning: 'I feel terribly upset that Kenny Watson should have been singled out in that game. There was so much going on in that game that deserved punishment, much of it before Watson even went on to the field. Yet he suffers. There were exceptional circumstances surrounding both of the ordering-off incidents!'

Yet, in a way, Waddell was not too unhappy about the atmosphere which had surrounded the two games.

He wasn't unhappy at the tough-guy tactics adopted by some of the German players, nor by the strange refereeing decisions, nor by the general difficulties faced by his players in the two games. He had wanted proper preparations for Europe. And he had got them!

He pointed out: 'This kind of thing goes on in football. You have to expect problems to be ·thrown up when you go into games against Continental clubs. They aren't meant to be picnics and we didn't take this trip as a rest cure. These young players we have must learn exactly how tough things can get in Europe. The quicker they do learn that the better it will be for them. I'm only disappointed that the trouble in the second game didn't allow me to play George Donaldson. It was no place for a youngster.'

The babes in the party had learned lessons and Waddell had been able to learn a few things, too. He had discovered that

Sandy Jardine was developing into a first-class right-back, that young Alfie Conn was maturing in his mid-field role, and that Bobby Watson had signs of being to top-class 'keeper. Also, there had been a new spirit about his team, the very fighting spirit and pride he had been trying to instil from the moment he took over control of the club.

In that sense, it has been a successful mission to Europe . . . and I suppose it wasn't surprising that when Waddell wanted a second refresher course in European football around Christmas then it was to West Germany that he took his team once again. Having been bundled out of European competition early by a single goal against the West German (again) cracks, Bayern Munich, Waddell wanted his youngsters to get another taste of Europe to consolidate their earlier lessons.

So, just before Christmas, the Rangers' party flew out to take on the toughest match schedule I have ever known any team accept travelling abroad. Waddell had decided that his team would play two games inside 24 hours against two teams from

Rangers' giant goalkeeper Peter McCloy rises confidently in this game against Falkirk at Brockville to clutch the ball safely. This was the kind of form that brought McCloy back into the team after he lost his place through illness on the pre-season trip to West Germany

the Bundesliga, Hertha of Berlin and Hanover 96. And, again,
Rangers were using the tour to work out tactics, to prepare
their players for the Scottish Cup games they would soon have
to face. They had had a run of indifferent League results and
had lost to St. Johnstone at Muirton just two days before leaving
for Berlin. Waddell wanted to try out changes. Tactical changes
and personnel changes. One of them was to bring the return of
Dave Smith, making his second comeback of the year in West
Germany.

Smith had dropped out of the first team following his earlier

The two visits to West Germany helped midfield man Dave Smith reach the kind of form which found him starring in the Cup victory over his former team Aberdeen. Here Smith, in mid-air, has tried a shot for goal with Willie Johnston the other Ranger in the picture. The Don's players are Henning Boel on ground and Jim Hermiston. Tragically Smith suffered another leg break near the end of the season

return in West Germany before the start of the season proper. Really, he had come back into the side too quickly following his leg break. He had needed more time to build both confidence and strength. Now he had been given that time and Waddell insisted that his artistry and skills were required by the team again, as one member of the middle three in a 4–3–3 line-up he wanted to experiment with in the giant Olympic Stadium in Berlin. Rangers did experiment with the new formation that night against Hertha but it all went for nothing, because as in the pre-season opener the Rangers lost an early

59

goal and struggled from then on. Defensive blunders in the second half finally tossed away any chance they had of saving themselves from defeat . . . or even making the defeat more respectable. They ended·the game losing 3–0. The first goal had been a penalty in just four minutes and the others had come inside nine second-half minutes after blunders by centre-half Ronnie McKinnon. It was no wonder that the lion rampant flags and banners held aloft by soldiers in the crowd were dangling limply and sadly in defeat long before the end.

It was a subdued party which flew out of the divided city of Berlin the next morning to head for Hanover and their second game. Subdued because they realised that they had let themselves down, and subdued, too, because they realised that their exhausting schedule called for them to play another game that night. I remember thinking how much better it would have been if the players had been simply heading for home after playing that single game in Berlin. The whole attitude and atmosphere seemed wrong after that Berlin defeat . . . yet that night in the Niedersachser Stadium I saw Rangers draw on all their fighting spirit to hit one of the peaks of their erratic form. They threw off the tiredness which must have been clinging to their every muscle. They hurled aside the dejection and disappointment that hung over them from their game in Berlin . . . and they went out to win! Two weeks earlier their Berlin conquerers, Hertha, had come to the same stadium and could only manage a draw . . . that in itself gave some measure of the Rangers' improvement.

Alfie Conn scored a glorious goal for them in ten minutes after a beautifully constructed passing movement between young left-back Alec Miller and John Greig.

Then 13 minutes from the end it looked as if the victory Rangers deserved was going to be snatched from them when Greig pushed a cross from the Hanover outside-right, Rudi Nafziger, past Peter McCloy and into the Rangers' goal. It would have been a tragedy if the win that Rangers had earned had disappeared that way . . . but somehow they pulled out their last reserves of strength and stamina to attack and attack again and before the end Alec Miller scored with a low shot to make the final result 2–1. It was a performance to be proud of.

Any team who can travel to West Germany and return home with a victory has accomplished something. To do that after already playing a match against top opposition just 24 hours earlier was really something special. Willie Waddell knew that. As we flew home the next morning he admitted to me: 'I didn't expect these players to shake off the disappointment they felt in Berlin as quickly or as successfully as they did for the game in Hanover. They had a hangover from the Hertha game. We all knew that . . . but they refused to give in to it. They went out there to get a result. They gave notice, some of these young players, that they accepted this responsibility as part of growing up in the game.'

Then, on the tactical ideas he had tried out, Waddell told me: 'Look, in the pre-season games we tried out tactics we intended to use in Scotland week after week. We didn't tighten things up at the back the way we normally would have done in games away from home especially when it came to competitive games.

'This time it was different. We came away from home to try tactics specifically designed for matches in Europe. We could have played matches against foreign opposition at home. There were half-a-dozen Continental teams who wanted to meet us at Ibrox . . . but that isn't what I wanted. I wanted to get abroad and have the players facing the type of conditions that they must face in competition when they are playing in the away leg of any European tie. Tactics can be tried out on practice grounds. Formations can be used in training games. But they cannot be tested properly or proved satisfactorily until they have been given a run in actual games. This is why we returned to West Germany.'

Besides getting the experience for Europe, Waddell also gained toughening experience for his players to prepare them for the vital Scottish Cup games ahead and saw Dave Smith make a studied return to the mid-field to provide the calming influence on the play there which had, at times, been too hurried.

Before Waddell went to West Germany he had realised better than anyone that his chances in the League had slipped away. He knew, therefore, that his best chance of further success to place alongside the League Cup victory, was in the Scottish Cup competition. And so the trip to West Germany had had a two-fold mission, preparation for the problems of Europe, and preparation for the Scottish Cup.

Once again the football fields of West Germany had become a vital training ground for Waddell and his new Rangers . . .

Sandy Jardine, the Rangers' star whose move to right-back saved his Ibrox career and took him into the Scotland team

SANDY JARDINE

The move which kept me a Ranger

LAST season could have been the one which ended my career as a Rangers' player. In fact, it would probably have done so if I had not managed to make a permanent first team spot for myself in a new position at right back!

I had made up my mind at the end of the previous season that I would try to get away from Ibrox if I hadn't made the grade in the first team. Not because I didn't like Rangers as a club, not because I had lost any of the tremendous feeling I had for them as a team to play for. But, simply because I felt that this was going to be my last chance to make something of myself as a full time professional footballer at Ibrox. I had been with Rangers for five years, constantly it seemed being shifted from one position to another, having spells in the first team and then suddenly finding myself back in the reserves. I had, in fact, become a player without a settled place in the League team, and without even a settled position no matter which team I was playing in with Rangers.

When I had first joined Rangers as a seventeen-year-old I had known first team football early, going into the team as a midfield man and holding my place in the team as we fought our way into the final of the European Cup Winners Cup in 1967. Everything then had looked so good for me. People pushed me forward for Under-23 honours, I seemed to be established in the Rangers' first team plans . . . and then it all changed. I was dropped from the first team and my whole world seemed to collapse. Now and again I was brought back in my midfield role and then I was transformed into a centre forward with both the reserve and the first teams.

I don't suppose it was my favourite position on the field but I stuck to it, had a fairish run in the League side, scored a few goals, and then went straight back into the second team when Colin Stein was signed for £100,000 from Hibs. Nothing seemed to go right for me then. So, when the end of season 1969–70 came along and I found myself back in the first team . . . now converted

63

into a *right back*. I decided that I would give myself just one more season to make the real break-through. I made up my mind that if I couldn't establish myself in the first team this time then I'd have to try a change of club and maybe be able to establish myself somewhere else. I had been around for a long time at Ibrox and had seen players, too many players, stay on with Rangers, probably knowing that they would never make the first team, but hanging on hoping and praying that there would be a change of luck. I didn't want to find myself in that role . . . so I made my decision. One more year. Just one year longer to win and hold down a first team place.

I'm only glad now that I was never forced to try to leave the club, glad that the change of position did carry me to the first team spot I wanted so desperately.

The way things turned out last season eventually meant even more to me than simply winning the Ibrox right back position. The move I made also brought the international chance that had seemed possible when I first hit the first team and had then vanished from my dreams.

It really had vanished, you know. All my dreams, all my hopes had become centred on one thing . . . getting into the Rangers' first team. I didn't think beyond that. And then, when I did get back into the League side at Ibrox, I was so thankful that, again, nothing else entered my mind. As far as I was concerned I had done all that I wanted to do when the Boss decided that I was the best right back at Ibrox.

When the other honours began to arrive. When I was named for the full Scotland International pool and played for a short spell against Denmark in the European Nations Cup game at Hampden; when I reached the Under-23 team, and then the Scottish League team, I began to realise just how much that switch of positions had meant to me. The step back into defence had changed the whole course of my career. . . . .

I had played my first-ever game at right-back about two years before my re-appearance in the first team, during a close-season tour of Denmark and Sweden. I was chosen to play in a friendly in a little Danish town called Aabenraa. That was the first time, but at the end of 69–70 season I had been playing at right-back regularly. In fact, the Boss had me play five games there in one hectic week. They were a mixture of first-team and reserve games just when the League programmes were being wound up. I enjoyed it. It was new. I looked on it as a bit of a challenge and although I realised there were different aspects of the game to be considered if I was playing at full-back regularly I felt from the

65

Here he is, Willie Johnston, the outside-left Sandy Jardine would hate to see leave Rangers. In this picture Johnston, extreme left, raises his arm in triumph after scoring a goal. Colin Stein hugs him while Alfie Conn runs over to add his congratulations

beginning that it was a job I could settle into.

But it was really the close season, and on tour again, that I felt I had been ear-marked by the Boss for the job in the first team. I had been one of the players asked to work almost all through the already short close season at sprints in Edinburgh under the coach, Jock Wallace, and a former professional sprinter and sprint trainer, Tom Patterson. These sprint sessions were ideal for me. I had always felt that I needed to brush up a little on my pace and so I worked pretty hard at it.

I reckoned, too, that it would be a tremendous help to me in the right-back position. A modern full-back must have pace and stamina for long runs into overlapping positions to help his forwards . . . then the runs back into defensive positions if something went wrong upfield. I worked and worked until Tom Patterson eventually entered me for one or two of the professional sprints at the various meetings in the Borders. I won one of the races there, a 220 yards' event, and that was another boost to my confidence.

Then came the tour games in West Germany and the final proof for me that I was going to get the first-team position when the season started. These two games in West Germany, against Hamburg and Kaiserslautern, and then a third pre-season game against Spurs at White Hart Lane were to be tough tests for me. I knew that, all right. In Hamburg for the first game I was facing a former German international winger, Charlie Dorfel, and then in London I faced Roger Morgan of Spurs—both of them were fliers. I doubt if it would have been possible to pick two more difficult customers than these two for the start of my new career. I felt really that I was still adjusting to the new position and it was hard going for me against them. But again the Boss must have been satisfied because I stayed in the team when the season proper opened.

I knew now that it was up to myself to justify the faith he had shown in me. I knew that I had to work hard to learn the proper approach to the new position, to try to read the different situations that a full-back must face. Of course, I had realised already that the role of a full-back has changed in recent years, probably more than the role of any other player in football.

It isn't enough any longer simply to be able to tackle hard and keep a winger out of the game as much as possible. For a start, it's not so very often these days that you have a winger directly opposed to you, especially when you start facing continental teams or even teams from England. In most countries the orthodox winger has died, though in Scotland we have been able to persist with wing play because we have good wingers. We use wingers at Ibrox, for instance.

Anyhow, the point I am trying to make is that when you are not faced with a winger who is carrying the ball at you, when you are probably faced with no direct opponent then your job can become as much an attacking as a defending job. It is up to you to overlap as often as possible, helping to set up attacks, forcing on play and giving the opposing team the problem of having to deal with an extra attacker. The whole business of overlapping has become an essential part of the full-back's playing equipment. Often the full-back is called upon to do the job that once belonged exclusively to the winger—going down the wing carrying the ball and then hitting the bye-line before putting a cross into goal.

You must work on this and to do so you must also work out an understanding with any winger who is playing in front of you. At practice games and training sessions at our Albion ground, Willie Henderson and myself often find ourselves trying out different moves which allow me to overlap without upsetting his play any. To benefit the team properly a back and a winger must get this thing going, and I think that we have managed to build an understanding. Willie knows when I am going to move upfield and I know, too, how he will position himself once I have succeeded in getting myself into an attacking situation.

Really, this wasn't the part of the new position that I found particularly difficult. Most of my previous playing experience had been in attacking roles, either right up front as a striker or in the midfield as a link man. Using the knowledge I had gained from these other jobs helped me as far as the attacking part of the full-back business went.

Where my problems arrived were in the strictly defensive duties. We employ the normal type of defensive system used by British teams at Ibrox. This calls for the full-backs to pivot infield on to the centre-half to provide extra cover at the centre of the defence. If an attack is building up on the left flank then I move inside a little and when the attack comes to my side of the field then it works the other way around. It gives depth to the defence and vital cover in danger areas. It gave me most of my problems at the start. I think that the Boss and Jock Wallace must have been hoarse shouting at me in those early games. Either I would not be pivoting enough or else I would be over-compensating on the pivot which led to other problems for the defence. These were my worst moments at the start until I gradually found that pivoting properly came once I had adjusted

67

to the position and become used to playing there.

Basically I look on myself as one of the school of modern full-backs because that's the way that I have been coached for the position and it's also the way the position appealed to me. I don't know if I would have been as happy at full-back if the role had been as defensive as it once was. I like to be involved in a game and a modern full-back has that distinct advantage. Of course, now that I have made the switch permanently I consider myself a right-back. Not a midfield player, and certainly no longer a 'utility' man. So I have found myself studying closely other full backs.

For instance, when I was first moved there and began to think about the chance I was going to perhaps get in the first team, I found myself watching the World Cup from Mexico on tele-vision. And I found myself watching the full-backs particularly closely. The games there provided me with the two players I have tried to model myself on since I changed over. They were the Brazilian captain, Carlos Alberto, and the Italian captain, Giacinto Facchetti. Both have the ideal qualities, in my opinion, for modern full-back play. They have the ability to come forward intelligently, combined with a sound defensive knowledge and the twin attributes I mentioned earlier of speed and stamina. If I can ever approach any of them then I will believe that I have really made it as a top-class full-back.

It's funny, of course, how your thinking becomes coloured by your own role in a team. For example, though I believe in wing play, in a team using good wingers, I'm quite happy to see the growth of the 4–3–3 set-up. Basically it is the lack of wingers in direct opposition to me that allows me the freedom that I enjoy most in the role—and without wingers the job has less problems!

In fact, I find the most difficult outside-lefts I have been asked to play against so far are both team mates of mine at Ibrox. One is the regular first-team man, Willie Johnston, whose speed is really fantastic, and the other is young Ian MacDonald. the kid we have nicknamed Dougal at Ibrox. Little Ian is brilliant. He has tremendous ball control and his dribbling is fantastic. He has given me more problems in practise games than anyone has ever managed to give me so far in competitive matches. Every time I come away from the Albion after one of these full-scale practice games I thank my lucky stars that Ian is a Rangers' player.

I would shudder at the prospect of having to face up to him in a competitive game. He is the most promising young player at Ibrox despite the dreadful run of injuries he has had to fight against.

Jardine slides into a tackle against Arthur Duncan of Hibs, the winger he claims gives him the most trouble outside his own club

Outside of the club I've probably been given my hardest time from Arthur Duncan of Hibs. If anyone happens to wonder why, then they have only to throw their minds back to the Under-23 international against England at Hampden last season when Arthur ran riot against the Englishmen. He was superb that night and, having had a taste of the medicine he can dish out, I sympathised with the poor English defenders who had the job of stopping him that night. When Arthur is in the mood he will worry the best full-backs in the world.

Fortunately, with the present trend in the game still leading away from wingers, I haven't too many more troublesome opponents. I just go along hoping it stays that way, allowing me to consolidate my position in the Rangers' first-team set-up—and perhaps do the same at Scotland level. When I look back on the past year I realise just how much of a heart break it would have been for me to have to leave Ibrox.

That's why I'm so glad that the switch to right-back gave me my first-team chance—and my chance to stay with the one club in the world that matters to me!

Another duel between Jardine and the outside left he rates so highly,
Arthur Duncan of Hibs. This time Jardine is at full stretch as he
tries to block a Duncan cross

Stan Anderson
Boss of the Babes

WHEN Stan Anderson was plucked from the relative obscurity of playing with Clyde to take over the job as coach to the reserve team at Ibrox, there were eyebrows raised in some areas of Scottish soccer.

Anderson had been admired as a skilled and thorough professional. But his career as a player had been far from glamorous and he had no real coaching experience to back him in his new job. Yet manager Willie Waddell, the man who made the appointment, saw qualities in Anderson that the doubters didn't. At least, qualities that they had not seen at the start of last season but qualities, which, by the end of the campaign were apparent to everyone. The same qualities which Anderson had used to mould a team of boys straight from school into a powerful reserve team.

He had been given charge of the youngest team in the Scottish Reserve League, but by his patient and complete coaching he guided them into the final of the Reserve League Cup and made them a team to be reckoned with in the League.

It was done by hard work and by determination, two qualities that Anderson and everyone at Ibrox demand from any players on the staff. The 32-year-old Anderson, whose career had taken him from Hamilton Acas to Rangers (yes, Rangers, even though he was eventually given a free transfer by the Ibrox club) back to Hamilton and then on to Clyde, is dedicated to the job he holds down.

You talk to him and you find yourself being carried along with him in his unquenchable enthusiasm for his favourite subject—his team, his youngsters, and the job they are doing on the field for Rangers.

Says Anderson: 'I have never been so happy as when I was told that I had been appointed to the job as reserve team coach at Ibrox. I had spent so much of my time in football as a part-time player, wishing that I could become a full-time player and spend all my time working at and thinking about football—and now

73

The man whose mission it is to groom the Ibrox babes . . . reserve team coach Stan Anderson

here was the chance that I had waited for. Not just that, it wasn't as if this was going to be something special just for myself, it was a job that was going to benefit young players. I thought that it might be a job of tremendous value and I suppose it captured my imagination a bit.

'The whole idea of training and coaching the youngsters appealed to me a lot. When I was a young player just coming into the game, the opportunities for this type of thing were very, very limited. Really, we were left to teach ourselves about the game. I'm going back ten years or maybe a little more than that, and then, we had to teach ourselves by experience. There wasn't any other way possible.

'Now it's different, thank goodness. There are more ex-players involved in coaching with the First Division clubs, especially, and ideas, hints, little things that we have picked up along the way can be passed on to the young players who are just coming into the game. We had to learn from mistakes we made—now these same mistakes might help a youngster mature a little quicker.

'It's a tremendous chance for me, of course, and what makes it even better is the fact that so many of the teenagers who come to Ibrox are prepared to work hard at the game. They *want* to learn and that makes the job so much easier.'

Anderson found that out early in his new career. Away back during his opening weeks in the job, during the opening weeks at Ibrox for so many of the young players he has worked with this past season, he discovered which players were willing to show the dedication and determination to learn that he wanted from them.

Smiling a little, he recalls: 'Before I got to know the lads properly, I used to test them out a little bit in these first weeks of training. I used to tell them after the morning work-out that we had nothing planned for the afternoon and that they could have the afternoon off. Then I would add that I was going to come back myself and if any of them felt like doing a little bit extra then they would be more than welcome. I wondered just how many of them would take up the invitation. You know, I had been working them hard all the morning even then. I might have understood if one or two of them thought they had done enough. But I don't have to tell you almost every single one of them turned up, they all wanted to keep on working. To me that showed how keen they were to get on in the game.'

This kind of opportunity was exactly the type of opportunity that Anderson didn't get himself. Specialised coaching wasn't part of a player's life then. Possibly it is for that reason he is now ready to spend so much time helping the kids who want so much to be helped. Yet he constantly plays down his own commitment. He would rather tell you how much easier his job is made because of the attitude that so many of the Ibrox babes have adopted. He sums up simply: 'It's easy to work with people who always want to get on with the job in hand.'

The teenagers at Ibrox want to work. They would not remain there too long if they didn't!

One of the reasons for their willingness is probably the example set by Anderson's own unflagging enthusiasm. Another is very definitely the openings that exist for the younger players under Manager Waddell's 'give youth a chance' policy. The number of players who have been promoted to the first team at various times throughout the season is a credit to the scouting system and to Anderson's hard work. But the chance of a first-team place is also a gigantic carrot dangled temptingly in front of every young player. They now *know* that if they work hard, if they show up well in the second team then a first team chance will come to them. They now *know* that they won't be overlooked when a first-team opening looms up. The team selections of the past season proved that repeatedly to them and to every Rangers' fan!

Anderson has worked hard, but clearly he has been helped and occasionally guided by assistant manager Willie Thornton and assistant trainer Joe Craven. Says Anderson: 'Mr. Thornton and Joe kept telling me that it would take time to get the youngsters adjusted properly to the more exacting training routines they were getting and also to the higher standard of football they were suddenly being asked to play in. At the start I was ready to take on the world. It was inexperience, in a way, I suppose, but the advice I kept getting helped me to see, at last, that I would hit problems that I hadn't even thought about.

'We were fielding the youngest reserve team in the whole League almost every week. That was a handicap in itself some of the time. I mean, no matter how much coaching we can give to a player there are certain situations he must face at some time on the field which he can cope with only through experience.

'These situations can only come sometimes in competitive games. It is only in a real game that the player has a chance to adapt himself to unexpected events.

'We had some disappointments in the season because of this, but we did a whole lot better than some people might have expected. After all, most of the players we had in the team had been playing in schools' football the previous season!'

One of the main tributes to Anderson and his team was the interest being shown in their progress by Rangers' fans right through the year. There was always some talk around the Stadium before the first-team games, of the promise shown by

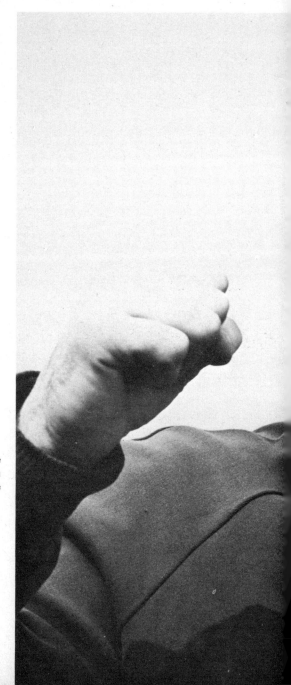

Some vocal encouragement for the youngsters at Ibrox from the man who handles their training, reserve team coach Stan Anderson

76

one youngster or another in the reserve side. Teenagers no one had heard of six months earlier were soon being talked about. George Donaldson, Alex Morrison, George Walker, Tom Alexander, Derek Parlane and especially Derek Johnstone became some of the names to be bandied about by the fans. It was a

change to hear so much interest being shown. There had been times in the past when reserve teams at Ibrox were looked on as soccer graveyards for players who would never quite make the grade—now there was a freshness and vitality about the team that the fans appreciated.

And in my interviews with Anderson, the young coach was eventually persuaded to give a few of his own personal tips for the top. Before going through the players he stressed, mind you, 'I don't have any favourites in this team. I'll name one or two players the general public might now know too much about, players I think, will make their mark. But they aren't the only players we have who will break through. Just wait and see. . . .'

Anyhow, here are the players Anderson mentioned, and the comments he made about each one: Forward Derek Parlane— 'I had a bit of a problem with Derek at the start because I felt he was a bit soft. He didn't shout much in games, didn't get too involved at times in some of the horseplay that goes on a bit in the dressing-rooms. Looking at all these things I felt I had to get a bit of devilment into him.

'He had ability, I knew that. But I wanted him to develop some hardness to go with that ability. As it was he was too easily knocked off the ball even in practise games. I brought him back to build his strength and to stress to him that he must be ready to give more physically. I had to hammer it into him that he shouldn't be shoved off the ball so easily by anyone. I think all the concentration on this part of his game has helped the boy.'

Midfield man Alex Morrison—'This is a player who has the kind of flair for the game that Jim Baxter had. Believe me!

'He was a bit on the small side when he came to us at first, so we had to work on buiding him up. He has grown almost an inch in his first year and we have tried to make sure that his strength has been spread evenly through his body. He has great ability, with his strongest point, quite naturally, as a creator. This boy can make something out of nothing on the field. Watch him this year. I think he will be a stand out for us.'

Forward George Walker—'George came to us from Drum-chapel Amateurs and, honestly, he is exactly the kind of lad we would look for at Ibrox. Naturally he has ability. That's taken for granted when a youngster comes along—but he has so much character too. I can illustrate that with a wee story about George when he was at Gullane for the special training we do there.

'George was working with the first-team lads on the course laid out by the coach, Jock Wallace. Now they were used to it, besides being older and probably stronger than George. But that made no difference to him. He was physically sick from his efforts almost half-a-dozen times that day and he refused to quit. Jock Wallace told him he had done well, that he should take a rest after he had done it three times. He wouldn't take a break. He just kept going—and every attempt he made he handed in a better time than he had done before.

'He simply wouldn't give in—he was so determined to succeed—and that's an attitude that you want. He was unlucky with injuries last year but he'll come through. He has phenomenal work rate, uses the ball well and can snap goals. He will be a good Ranger.'

Midfield man, George Donaldson—'This boy is a natural. He is good in the tackle, good in the air and can play so much football with it all. During the season there he had a stationary period when we could see a slight falling off, reaction to training, perhaps. Anyhow, he has passed that now and he finished as strongly as when he started. He had to be nursed a little bit in training, but with boys practically straight from school this has to be done for a lot of the lads.'

Right-back Tom Alexander—'Tom·isn't the classiest player we have in the reserves, but what an honest-to-goodness lad he is. He is utterly dedicated to the game, would work all day if you asked him and he can tackle well and come forward, too. He is the kind of boy who is so hungry for success and so determined to make the grade that it would be difficult to see him fail.'

Forward Derek Johnstone—'Derek, of course, broke through to make the first team for a fairly lengthy and successful spell. In fact he knocked in goals for them just the way he was doing it for us. He is brilliant in the air and coming on well on the deck, too. I think he will become a great player. He looks a little bit slow at times but we have him working out with spikes and trying sprint starts which are bound to help his pace. Once he develops the instinct for proper positioning—again that is something that can only come with experience—then he will be a top class striker.'

After these brief assessments of some of its budding stars he handles and nurses so carefully Anderson went on to outline some of his training ideas.

'We always try to have the lads coming in to something new every day,' he explained. 'It's no use letting them come in knowing exactly what they will be doing. There has to be a constant element of surprise.

'For example, we try to let all the players see how the other half lives so to speak. By that, I mean that we mix the lads up

Striker Derek Johnstone of Rangers shows the brilliance in the air that Stan Anderson talks about. Here he outjumps two much more experienced players in Doug Smith, left, and Stuart Markland, right, of Dundee United, Johnstone's home town team

a little bit when we are playing in the practice games. We ask defenders to become attackers and vice versa. This way a defensive player can find himself in a situation which is new to him. A situation that is normally applicable only to attackers. They have to react to this and in doing so get some idea of how an opponent might think and act during a game. We try to do this fairly often. It allows the lads to get a proper picture of the game, to be able to assess things not just from their own specialist positions but from *any* position. I believe it gives them a better understanding of the game.

'At this stage we lay our main emphasis on the basic skills of the game. It isn't really possible to delve too deeply into the tactical aspects of the game. Naturally, we give the players basic formations to use on the field and we work out other things, too. We might set players up in certain positions that will arise during games and demonstrate what positions others players should take up even when they may not be directly involved in the play.

'All the time, though, we try to insist that they keep the game simple, as simple as possible. We all believe that football is an easy game if played properly and we drive this into them all the time. We tell them to try to do the easy thing, the natural thing and then we can add to that later.'

There is another aspect, too, that Anderson insists is essential to success with his youngsters. He emphasises: 'I try to tell them all the time that they are Rangers' players and I try to hammer home exactly what that means. Being a Ranger is an achievement for any player . . . and they have to live up to the reputation and traditions of the club. We want to instil a pride in the club in these boys right from the start. It's all part of the process of getting players ready for the first team . . ."

Anderson had a reasonable success last year working to these principles. Predictably, though, he won't rest on any laurels he might have gained. He says: 'We did all right, but we can do better and we will do better. I've been learning with the lads to a certain extent and I've been lucky in that I've been guided by Mr. Waddell and Mr. Thornton and Jock Wallace and Joe Craven. I've learned about handling youngsters from them and I couldn't have asked for more help. . ."

The babes feel the same about Stan Anderson.

Jock Wallace demands effort from his Rangers' squad at training . . .

JACK WALLACE

Training
the Wallace Way

MY MAIN AIM in this article is to provide a basic coaching
course which can be easily followed by youngsters. There is
nothing advanced here, nothing that can only be attempted
by experienced senior players. This is a guide for the younger
player who wants to improve his all-round ability, and it
naturally includes some hints from the coaching sessions we
have at Ibrox.

To work on the basic individual skills I have broken the
article into five specific parts and will deal with each of these
five at some length. This is the way I would approach the job
of coaching a group of youngsters and, therefore, I hope that
it can be of some benefit to those among you who want to
learn about the game . . . and who want to get better at the
game, too!

One—BALL CONTROL—I use the very general heading of 'ball
control' here although really, parts of this come into the other
parts of the article. Still I reckon it deserves to have something
devoted to it alone. Let's face it, you cannot do very much
in the game, or go very far, if you don't have the basic control
of the ball. Now, when a young player reports to Ibrox for the
first time you expect him to have this essential quality in his
make-up. But possessing ball control doesn't give anyone the
automatic right not to continue working on their control
until it is almost perfect. We hammer this first principle of
soccer all the time in our training sessions, hammer it to the
youngest and least experienced players, right through to the
lads who have been with the club for years, who have won
international honours and played in Europe. Because I believe
that you must keep working hard at this, never letting up on it
for a moment.

One simple way to do this, and we do it at Ibrox, is to have
the youngsters hitting a ball against a wall. Our lads do this
against the wall under the stand almost every morning in life
when they come in for training.

83

They hit that ball as hard as they can against the wall and then wait for it to come back to them. Naturally from a rough wall surface the ball can come back to them at a variety of heights, angles and speeds and the players must be able to bring it under control and lay it off quickly. This is technique training at its lowest level. All you need is a ball and a wall . . . and the capacity for concentration and hard, hard work.

When you work your way up towards the more experienced players then you have to try to vary the training routines according to the individuals. You have to have them working at speed, holding the ball under close control to make ground with it, passing it either with the inside or the outside of the foot, killing it and moving it on almost in the same movement. All of these have to be worked on . . . but at the start the wall game is the simplest exercise of all. And it is also tremendously effective.

For players with excellent ball control I always hold up as examples Bobby Charlton of Manchester United, Bobby Murdoch of Celtic and our own Andy Penman. Charlton, in particular, is an excellent example for any young players just heading into the game.

Two—PASSING—This follows on from the basic ball control that I have just covered. But there are various other points that you must bring home to a player, points which only apply to passing. For instance, the first essential is to impress on a player that you pass the ball only when YOU want to pass it. You must never allow yourself to be pressured into making a pass by the opposition. When they can force you to move a ball on when you are not ready then they are at an advantage. And you are more likely to make a mistake when you are being pressured, anyhow. Then, also, when young players come into Ibrox at the very start of their careers with the club they often fall into the same trap. They make a pass in a game and then think that their job is over. What we have to get them to realise is that making the pass is just the start of their job. . . .

You cannot simply make a pass and then stand around waiting to see what the other player is going to do with the ball. You have to keep on the move all the time, trying to run into space, making yourself available for the return ball. A pass only starts a move, and the ultimate aim of any move is a goal, or, at least, a try at goal. There is no time to stand still in a game and so the players have to be told to keep moving, keep backing up the player who has possession, finding space and being ready for a return ball if it is on. The main way you can develop this in players is by playing one touch or two touch football in the practice games. We have a go at this almost every day in training. Again it is simple, and can be done by any group of youngsters. It gets over to them exactly what you want. If a player is limited to two consecutive touches of the ball then he must be ready to release the ball quickly and move just as quickly into position for a return pass from a team-mate. When they are not allowed to hold the ball for any length of time then they begin to think more quickly about what they must do and about how well they can do it.

Three—HEADING—This is another important aspect of the game and it falls into three categories, defensive heading, striking heading and directional heading. The last of the three is naturally incorporated in both of the others and with some great importance in each one.

A defender's main job with a header is to get the ball clear. He must not simply get up there for a ball and let it bounce off his head. He must go up and put power into any clearance header. At the same time he must also be able, on occasions, to head for a certain target. This is where directional heading comes into it, where a defender is in a crowded goal area and has to look for a team-mate, head it to him and allow him to clear the ball because he is in a better position to do so.

A great deal of the success of a defensive header depends on the timing involved. A player must time his jump properly and to do that he must be able to judge perfectly the last foot of the ball's flight. It is that last foot that is important if a player is going to get real power behind the ball when he makes impact. That power is necessary in both types of defensive heading. If the defender is making a straight-forward clearance then he must have power behind the ball to carry it well upfield. If he is making a directional header to a colleague in the clear then he must still make that header with authority. They must have this authority even when the defender is being placed under pressure from the opposition. We try to simulate this by having other players jumping against them in tight situations during training.

For an example of a defender who has tremendous directional powers I simply cannot go beyond our own sweeper Colin Jackson at Ibrox.

Striking heading doesn't vary so very much. Again proper

Stan Anderson prepares to take the throw and Jock Wallace makes his first move towards 'defender' Tom Craig

This is a series of six photographs in which Rangers' coach Jock Wallace demonstrates the basic method of finding space for himself at a throw-in. The throw is being taken by assistant coach Stan Anderson, with Wallace being marked by physiotherapist Tom Craig

Wallace has made his feint to the right with Craig covering him as the throw is almost on the way . . .

Now comes the change of direction just before the throw is made. Wallace turns quickly to move clear of Craig who is caught on the wrong foot

Wallace moves towards the ball which is now well on the way to him from Anderson's throw as Craig, the mock opponent, is left trailing

Wallace has succeeded in 'making space' for himself. He is in the clear as he rises to head the ball back to Anderson as Craig stands undecided between them

Craig has now been forced to follow the ball back to Anderson and Wallace is busy 'making space' once more. He illustrates one more important point here. Now that he has made his headed pass he is ready to move into the open again to provide a target for Anderson timing is essential and direction is even more important here than in defence. A striker must be able to head the ball with complete accuracy because so often he is given only the tiniest of targets to aim at. Again, a simple point, but an important one when dealing with young players, these striking headers must be done with the players' eyes wide open. A player must have looked at where he is trying to place the ball, whether it is into the goal or into a gap in the box where he is trying to find one of his team-mates. Bravery comes into this because a striker must have courage to go for so many of these balls as they come into the penalty box.

For me Wyn Davies of Newcastle United and Wales is the best example of a striker who can do all these things. He climbs so well, gets above the ball really, and then snaps his head and gets real power behind any header he makes. Our own Derek Johnstone is another player who is developing this way. His headed goal against Moscow Dynamo in the game at Ibrox was a perfect example of a striking header.

A simple exercise for youngsters is to hang balls at various heights from the roof of a gym and then set them moving at different speeds and get the lads trying to time their jumps. We use this idea at Ibrox. It helps the timing of the jump and by raising the balls slightly at times you can improve the height of the players' jumping as well.

Four—MAKING SPACE—This is one of the most important aspects of play in the modern game. Because of defensive attitudes in the game today players find themselves being forced more and more into tight situations and they cannot find the room they need to make a positive contribution to their own team's tactics. What a player must be able to do in these circumstances is to make space, to get in the clear, away from his opponent and then be able to accept a pass from a team-mate.

In the modern game wingers must be made more aware of the uses of space and running into space than they ever were before. They must be ready to go inside, sometimes only as a decoy, to allow room on the flanks for a full-back to run into space. At Ibrox we have Sandy Jardine who must be able to time his run upfield so that it carries him into a clear area, into space where he can create the maximum amount of danger to the opposition. If he doesn't shake off the opposition completely he can still pull a man out of the middle of the field to cover him and that leaves space in the vital area around their goal. A player may not always get the benefit of these runs himself . . . but the team can still benefit. This is important to stress to young players. A great deal of damage can be done by a player who is willing to run into space even though he may never get possession of the ball.

You can also make space for yourself by using the quick one-two pass, or the wall pass as it is sometimes called. This is where you give the ball quickly to a team-mate and then move away from whoever is marking you to take the return.

This can be done at speed and if it is done properly then it puts the opposing defence at a disadvantage. Again this is something that we work on at training.

It is one of the more difficult jobs in football coaching to teach young players the value of finding space. Most players coming from school still tend to think that the important work is all done ON the ball. We have to demonstrate to them how much damage can be done OFF the ball.

A simple way of illustrating how to make space for yourself on the field is to set up three players for a throw-in, one to take the throw, one to accept the ball and one to do the marking. You then show a youngster how to feint one way and then move quickly the other way to allow yourself room to gather the ball from the throw. Again, this is going back to training at its simplest . . . but, again, too, it is an effective way to get it over to teenagers. This is part of the game that develops with experience but you must also have application from the players. They have to be ready to work at the various ways of improving their running power off the ball.

For examples here I would suggest that the players youngsters should look at include Tommy Gemmell of Celtic, Alan Ball of Everton, and, of course, Bobby Charlton.

Five—SHOOTING—This is practised three or four times every week at Ibrox because we believe it is vitally important for our players. And when I say 'our players' like that, I mean all of our players. Every single man on the staff is given shooting practice. We have players from every position taking part for the very simple reason that you never really know when a player who may normally be a defender will suddenly find himself in a shooting position. If this situation occurs during a game then you want the player involved to have had the same benefits of shooting practice as any of the others have had.

In the usual training routine we have the players lined up and coming into the shooting area while myself and Stan Anderson send in various balls for them to have a crack at.

The quiet word of encouragement as Jock Wallace tries to coax
more from young Alfie Conn during a training session

We give them all kinds of passes, cut backs from the bye-line, square balls, hard, soft, along the ground, lobs, you name it and we include it at some stage of this exercise. We may also bring in someone else to provide lay-off headers for the player coming onto at speed. We try to cater for every possible situation that might arise during an actual game. In fact, with the speed we work at in this part of the training, then I would reckon that in half an hour a player can have more shots at goal from more different situations than he would run up against in six or seven competitive matches. We keep them under pressure all the time here. Again there can be no time for slacking. They have to keep going and keep going at speed!

For this aspect of the game I would advise young players to study Bobby Charlton, whose power and accuracy are fantastic, Joe McBride of Dunfermline, Harry Hood of Celtic and from our own men at Ibrox John Greig and Andy Penman.

I suppose you have noticed by now just how often I have held up Bobby Charlton as an example in the various aspects of the game I have covered. I make no apologies for this. I rate Charlton as highly as I rate any player in the game. He is absolutely tremendous and one of the ideal types of player,

An angry-looking Jock
Wallace lays down the
law to Colin Jackson
(back to the camera) as
other Rangers' players
look on at the Albion
training ground

the type that any club manager would like to have on his
books. He has all the skills that I have mentioned and besides
that he has an off-field attitude that young players would do
well to try to emulate. This man Charlton has been a credit to
the game and I think that this is an important thing to stress
when you are coaching youngsters. He has been thoroughly
professional both on and off the field right through his career.
When you have a man like that around you know that you
will always be able to depend on him.

He typifies the type of character we want to have at Ibrox.
We want players with a good attitude off the field, players
with a good background. We want them to be professional on
the field and a credit to the club when they are away from
football, too. I demand respect from the players under me
and I want to be able to give that respect back to them. We
don't want any bad types in the club. No matter how well they
may be able to play . . . we just don't want them. They must
be Rangers on and off the field. Our aim is professionalism
and I believe strongly that behaviour away from the club is
part of that. There is no better example to hold up to a young
player than Bobby Charlton. . . .

Diary of a
Soccer Starlet

ALEX MORRISON is slim, freckled and eighteen years of age. He was a schoolboy star at that well-known soccer breeding ground Clydebank High School, the same school which produced Bobby Hope and Asa Hartford of West Bromwich Albion and Aston Villa's centre-forward Andy Lochhead. Later he played for Rangers' best known nursery team, Drumchapel Amateurs. Then last year he was called up to Ibrox as a full time professional and that year was one which changed his whole life.

Suddenly he was playing alongside soccer stars he had so recently hero-worshipped from the steep terracings of Ibrox. Suddenly he was asked to cope with the rigorous training schedules that quickly turned him from a schoolboy into a man. Suddenly, too, in his native Clydebank, he was no longer a little-known juvenile player . . . he was Alex Morrison of Glasgow Rangers.

There are times when these changes can upset any youngster, but Morrison was one of the Ibrox crop who remained comparatively unaffected by all the glamour of the move. If anything he stayed as starry-eyed as he was on the first day he reported for training as a full-time Rangers' player.

Towards the end of that first season I spoke to him and he gave me the following insight into the life of a star babe with Rangers. . . .

'It is still difficult for me to believe it all at times when I look around the dressing-room and see someone like Willie Henderson standing alongside me. You see, when I was first allowed to go to the games at Ibrox when I was a boy Wee Willie was my idol. He was the greatest as far as I was concerned.

'He was just pushing his way into the team then, taking over from Alex Scott and making that right-wing position his own at the age of seventeen. He wasn't just a hero to me, he was the hero of every schoolboy who were on the terracings

95

A portrait of Rangers' babe Alex Morrison, one of the
teenagers whose lives have been changed by signing for the great
Ibrox club

with me. He seemed almost one of us and we seemed to try to identify with him from our place in the ground.

'Anyhow, here I am now, playing for Rangers myself, and playing alongside Wee Willie in the practice games and sweating it out with him on the sand dunes at Gullane . . . it's a whole new world and I think all the young lads in the reserve team feel exactly the same way about it as I do at times.

'The most wonderful thing about Ibrox today is that you are treated almost as an equal with the first team squad from the very beginning. There is no segregation of the reserves from the first team, you are all in there together, doing the same kind of training and playing in the same practice matches.

'Naturally there must be times when we are working out separately, for instance, if the first team squad are preparing specifically for an important game and everything is being concentrated on that. But the usual routine, the policy of the club, has us all working as one big family of players. You feel a part of the club right from the start.

'I know that's how I felt when I was beginning as a full-time player. Initially, when you are approaching the ground on that first morning you feel nervous. I'm sure that's the same for everyone. You don't really know what to expect once you do start. It's a big change to come from schools' football, with just a taste of amateur football as well and then find yourself walking up to Ibrox as a Rangers' player!

'Just walking through that front door and seeing the marble staircase and the chandeliers and all the rest of it gives you butterflies right away. But, once you get into the dressing-rooms and start mixing with the rest of the players that starts to disappear. There's no way, really, that you can stay nervous when all the players are doing what they can to make you feel at ease. I'll always stay particularly grateful to Alfie Conn and Alex MacDonald who were especially helpful to me at the start. No one, though, was ever big time to me. You are a Rangers' player like everyone else and that's the way you are treated.

'The first thing that strikes you when you join the Rangers is the thoroughly professional attitude that is adopted in their training methods. Every detail is looked after, every tiny problem that may arise is taken care of. The training staff concentrate on things that at school or with the amateur club would have been ignored. The little things are important to them because all of them count to make you into the kind of player they want. Of course, the entire training programme is carefully worked out. There is so much thought put into the schedules, and that simply could not happen at the lower levels of the game.

'You find out very quickly, too, that to get any praise at Ibrox from the training staff then you have to go some. I don't think you are ever allowed the luxury of believing that you have had a good game. I've seen myself coming in after a match and thinking that I'd done really well. You know, players can get this feeling themselves that they have had a good game. You kind of feel it in your bones and you come off that park feeling pretty pleased with yourself.

'Then, when you hit the dressing-room any chance of you getting big-headed about the performance ends. You find out there that your idea of what constitutes a good performance is quite a bit different from Stan Anderson's idea. You see, Stan is always able to point out mistakes that you have made. They might not be major errors, but even the smallest mistakes can land your team in trouble.

'You have probably been carried away thinking about the nice things that you have done . . . but the kind of post mortem Stan comes up with brings you right back to earth. It also makes you determined that the next time you play you won't be making the same mistakes he has picked you up on.

'As I said earlier the youngsters at Ibrox do the same training as the experienced first team men. And a fairly typical day goes like this:

'At ten o'clock we report to the ground to start training. We get stripped and then usually go on out into the gym for a game of head tennis before the training starts in earnest. The hard work starts just after ten o'clock when we all head out onto the track.

'We usually begin the track work with five minutes or so jogging, just to loosen up and then we split into squads for sprints, six consecutive 220's with special times demanded from us before we start. We could be asked to do the first one in twenty-eight seconds and then whittle that time down to twenty-six seconds by the time we do the sixth one. When I went at first I was doing the first one at around thirty seconds but gradually you get your times down, though its a slow process. After each sprint is over you resume jog trotting until the next one is called. You are never allowed to hang around on the track doing nothing, you have to keep moving.

'After the sprints are over you move onto what are called shuttle runs, short sharp dashes over ten yeards or so. These are important in football because so often you need the extra speed over these first, vital few yards when you are going for a ball. After this we might round off the track work with a short, quick session over the low hurdles.

'That can take up around forty minutes of the morning and then for twenty minutes or so we go on to work out on Jock

An action shot of Alex Morrison in a reserve game at Ibrox . . .

Wallace's circuit in the gym where he has all kinds of weight training devised for us. This was the killer for me when I started because it was so unlike anything that I'd ever been asked to do before. The very first time I did the circuit I was physically sick because of the exertion and strain it places on your body. Again, though, in time you became used to it. This is high pressured training but it builds your strength tremendously.

'The next part of the training is ball work, passing, shooting, heading, all the other basic skills are worked on and then we usually finish up with a practice game. That is a fairly typical morning work out but in the afternoon most of the younger players, like myself, are back at Ibrox to brush up on the skills of the game. We have different afternoons when we go back but the work done then is the same . . . specialist training for the individual when faults are worked on and strong points are improved.

'That is the picture of a basic day's work out but it isn't exactly what we do every day. Jock Wallace varies the routine all the time, he refuses to stick to a rigid daily training pattern.

'One day Jock will throw in something completely different, something we've never done before. Another day he'll stick to ball work all the time, another day he might give us longer on the weight training circuit.

'Jock believes that we should never be reporting for training knowing exactly what we will be doing each day. He maintains that a rigid routine breeds boredom and that isn't good for footballers.

'I must say that all of us appreciate this approach. Its good to have a change and we like it. In fact, I can't think of anything worse than reporting every morning and KNOWING that you are going to do the same old thing. Besides the obvious differences in the training from the amateurs to the professionals there is also a gulf in the playing standards. The main difference here lies in the work you are asked to do off the ball. In the lower grades of football you can make a good pass and then think that your job is over. As the saying goes, you "stand back and admire the pass", once it has been made. Now, in senior football you simply can't make the pass and then relax after the ball is away . . . you have got to back up that pass. Your job then is to get into a position to support the man to whom you've passed the ball. You must be prepared to take a return pass or at least provide him with another alternative move before he decides to release the ball.

'Again, when you make a pass, you find that you don't just stroke the ball or roll it along the ground to a team-mate. You have to rap the ball firmly, make it move quickly because everything in the senior grade is done at a much faster pace than the other grades.

'Away from the ground you find that your private life changes a bit, too. I feel now in Clydebank that everyone is looking at me, everyone is kind of pointing to me when I walk down the street because now I'm a Rangers' player. You see, I know so many people in Clydebank and this is just the way it has been. Rangers carries that special glamour in the very name of the club. It doesn't bother me too much. I don't think it has changed me any at all. I still have the same mates as I did when I was at school.

'We do the same things, too, though I suppose now I'm not out as much as I used to be. You have a lot of hard work to do in training and even more when you have a game so there's no point in having nights out and then feeling tired the next morning. You adjust to this.

'Everyone thinks about the good life that a footballer has, they talk about the £100 a week and the big cars and all the glamour but you don't have any of that when you are starting off on a football career. What you do have is hard work . . . and plenty of that! Mentally and physically you are being prepared for your career and you don't have so very much more money than any other youngster of your own age. What you do know, however, is that if you work hard and make the grade then there is big money to be earned and a good life to be had.

'I play in midfield and so, naturally, when I get to thinking about my career then I find myself thinking about other midfield players and trying to model myself on them a little bit. When I first went to Rangers my weakest spot was my tackling because I liked to push the ball about in the middle and not challenge too often. Anyway, the trainers worked on that. For one whole week they used me in practice games solely as a marker, just picking up one player from the start of the match, and going with him everywhere on the field. I had to go with him, tackle him and if I won the ball just get rid of it and pick him up again. They wanted me to curb my natural attacking instincts and improve on the tackling and it's coming better now.

'My ideal players, though, have remained the same, whether

I'm with Drumchapel Amateurs or Rangers and they are the West German international star Franz Beckenbauer of Bayern Munich and the Eire international player, Johnny Giles of Leeds United. When I was with Drumchapel I used to try to play like Giles all the time.

'He is always in the open space for Leeds, always available to take a pass and then he uses the ball magnificently. Everything goes through Giles when Leeds go on the attack and he is a real players' player.

'Beckenbauer is another great, great player. I just love watching him move with the ball. He is so elegant. It is magic just to watch him in action.

'At Ibrox I admire little Alex MacDonald. Sometimes a whole lot of the good things he does in a game are not fully appreciated by the fans . . . but what a player he is to play alongside. He helped me a lot when he was in the reserve team at the start of the season. . . .

'Then there is John Greig as well, the captain at Ibrox. He was with us in the reserves for a few games when he was shaking off an injury. Again John is a tremendous player to have alongside you in a team because he can be such an inspiration. He is always encouraging the other players and always driving the game on, too.

'I only really have one ambition of course and that's to make the first team at Ibrox. I suppose I've always wanted that ever since I was going to watch them as a school kid, and it hasn't changed any since I've joined the club. Like a lot of other Scots' lads I could have gone to England. Coventry were one team who made a firm signing offer and some others were interested but I had seen that Rangrs were starting to give youth a chance and I've never regretted joining up at Ibrox. I've spoken to players I know who have gone south and Rangers can stand with any club down there as far as treatment of young players goes. You do get a chance at Ibrox. I made a substitute spot on the bench once last season, and other young players were in the League side.

'This is a positive kind of encouragement for every young player at Ibrox. It lets all of us know that the club are watching you closely as you try to develop as a player. And I think that sums up the whole outlook of the staff at Ibrox . . . they watch over their young players. They guide us on and off the field and I don't think any of us would ever dream of playing anywhere else.'

Rangers' wonder boy centre forward soars high above Dundee
United goalkeeper Hamish McAlpine as team-mates Colin
Jackson, left, and Willie Henderson, right, watch. This is Derek
Johnstone trying to emulate his high flying heroes, Wyn Davies
and John Toshack

Moscow Dynamo
Then and Now

THERE is just just one thing that nourishes a Rangers' supporter more than success . . . and that is nostalgia. Well, success returned to Ibrox last season and so did nostalgia. They came within weeks of each other as Rangers first of all won the League Cup in the final against Old Firm rivals Celtic at Hampden Park and then, when the Ibrox team brought back to life one of the legendary games of the club's long and proud history.

It was a November night at Ibrox when the Russian club Moscow Dynamo returned to play a game which marked the twenty-fifth anniversary of the original meeting between the two great clubs of Scotland and Russia. And it was a night which reeked with memories of the past . . . and yet, strangely, was decided by what can only be called an omen for the future.

It was only a friendly game. But it had all the glamour of a great occasion in soccer. More than sixty thousand fans crowded into Ibrox to welcome the new Russian team, a side which was at that moment tied for the Russian First Division championship which they lost a few weeks later in a play off. That gave a hint of their standing as the fans rolled up, many of them recalling the first classic struggle, others, too young to remember that game themselves, listening with rapt attention to the tales of the famous Russian goalkeeper Tiger Khomich, the personality player of 1945, and of how the Russians tried at that time to sneak an extra player onto the field until the redoubtable Torry Gillick spotted the trick!

There were tangible links with the past, too. The Russian team manager Konstantin Beskov had been captain of the Dynamo team in 1945 and the Rangers' manager Willie Waddell had been outside right in the Ibrox team that day. Also there was the Rangers' skipper for the match, Jock 'Tiger' Shaw, who is now a member of the ground staff at Ibrox. Shaw led out the Rangers' team that night, renewing acquaintance with Beskov, meeting the Dynamo goalkeeper Lev Yashin who missed the match through injury, and awakening even more of the memories on the terracings.

Later I spoke to Shaw about the team he had played against and then to teenager Derek Johnstone whose goal gave Rangers their victory in the revenge fixture. It brought an interesting comparison and showed that though styles may have changed over the years, the national Russian characteristics of discipline and determination remained unchanged.

Jock Shaw, now 57, spoke first. He told me: 'That second game brought back so many memories for me and I suppose for our supporters, as well. It was such a fantastic occasion that first match in 1945, you know. It was just after the war had ended and people had been starved of football for years and now here was this glamorous game against a team from Russia. They were an unknown quantity to everyone in Scotland . . . including ourselves. Few people had even heard of them until they arrived in Britain and so there was this added mystery to the whole affair.

'At that time there weren't the games against European teams the way there are now. Nowadays a team coming from Europe is fairly common . . . then it was something extra special. And nothing could be more special than a team from Russia. I can still remember the crowds standing in huge queues in the centre of Glasgow and outside Ibrox, too, looking for tickets. Even now I don't think I can remember a game which brought such reaction from the public. Yet, when we had been told by the manager, Mr. Bill Struth, that we were going to be playing this game none of us had been too excited at the prospect. We didn't know anything at all about the playing standards in Russia. We didn't know any of their players and until we were told the game was arranged we weren't too interested in Russian football, either!

'The first time we were told we were playing them most of us thought that this would be an easy game for us to win. We had to change our minds about that when the Russians began their British tour.

'They played a strong Chelsea team at Stamford Bridge and drew 1–1, then they moved on to Cardiff and beat Cardiff City 10–1, and so by the time they arrived in Scotland we knew that we had a game on our hands. We also knew that we wanted to win, we wanted to give them their first defeat of the tour.

'Just before the game Rangers had bought Jimmy Caskie

from Everton. It was a genuine transfer deal and Caskie was to become a Rangers' regular . . . but the Dynamo officials refused to allow him to play against them. They were convinced that our only reason for getting Caskie was to have him play against them as a guest and then he would return to England. It wasn't that way at all but they simply refused to agree to allow Caskie to take the field in the game. They were so determined that they threatened to call the whole match off if Caskie did play. Rangers were within their rights to play him but because of the build-up the game had received, because of the advance ticket sales and because they didn't want a major row with the Russians, they finally agreed to the Dynamo demands. We went into the game without our new star signing.

'Looking back at the game now—and the return match there brought back so many memories—I realise that that game brought the first of the tactically-minded Continental teams to Ibrox. Nowadays the fans and the players are used to teams coming to play the game in a rigid tactical formation for a European Cup tie. They use "sweepers" and have their defence very tight and rely on quick breaks out of defence for all their attacks. It's commonplace today.

'But these were exactly the tactics Dynamo employed against us twenty-five years ago and we had never come up against them before.

'There was a precision about them that was unusual in a football team. You have got to remember that we played pretty much off the cuff at that time. The game had not developed tactically as it has today and so they took us by surprise. There was almost a military touch about them the way that they stuck to the playing system they had been given. It made things difficult for us but we did eventually draw 2–2 . . . and Willie Waddell had missed a penalty in the opening minutes. We came close to winning the game and it was a great, great match to play in and to watch. No one who was there will tell you anything else.

'At that time the Rangers pioneered the idea of playing teams from abroad and not too long after that Dynamo game we were in Portugal playing Benfica in Lisbon. That was fifteen years before most people in Britain had even heard of the famous Portuguese team.

'Still, the Dynamo game was the first. I suppose, in a way, even allowing for the earlier results, they surprised us by their ability. They went on to play one more game and surprised an 105

Rangers' young centre forward Derek Johnstone heads the ball
past the Moscow defence to score for Rangers. Player jumping
with Johnstone is Zykov. Moscow and the goalkeeper in black
is Smirnov watches the ball go into the net

Arsenal team packed with guest stars even more. Arsenal were allowed to play Stanley Matthews and Stan Mortensen and Joe Bacuzzi from Fulham and still lost 4–3.

'The Dynamo team had a lot of good players but the man the fans really took to as a personality was their goalkeeper Tiger Khomich. He was tremendously agile, like so many Continental 'keepers, and he had a fine game against us. Then the fellow who came back as the manager, Beskov, he was the inside-left, big and strong and lots of ability with it. The other outstanding man was the centre-half, who was really a modern-day "sweeper", Semichastny. He stayed back behind his defence and we had a lot of problems getting round behind him. It always gave me a laugh to hear how Inter Milan were the first team to use a "sweeper" when we came up against one way back a few months after the war was over!

'There were some amusing memories from the game, too. How the Russians played with long, long pants, longer than anything Alex James wore, I reckon. And they were embroidered round the bottom with big stripes that looked really funny to us and the fans. Then, at the start, they came up to shake hands and handed me a huge boquet of flowers. I still remember how embarrassed I was as the fans laughed and whistled at me. I remembered, too, going up Buchanan Street to get the bus home and the photographers chasing me and me trying to hide the flowers behind my back. Again it was so unusual, so different and it really earned me a bit of kidding.

'After the game at the reception the Russians were a bit reserved. Maybe they weren't too happy that Torry Gillick had caught them out at a bit of sharp practice during the game. You see it was another first for us . . . the first substitute! Only when the Russians put a player onto the field that day they didn't bother taking anyone off. At first the referee, Bobby Calder, who is now Aberdeen's chief scout, didn't spot the extra man. It took Torry Gillick to see what had happened and he counted the players and then pointed out to Bobby Calder that the Dynamo had TWELVE men on the field against us.

'All of these things are still talked about and I'm sure they will always be talked about by the Rangers' fans. The second game will have stories of its own about Derek Johnstone's header which brought the goal. At the same time it helped bring our own game back to life for so many of us.

'I must say that I appreciated being given the chance to go out onto the field before the game again with the Russian manager and Yashin. I was really touched by that gesture from Willie Waddell. He didn't tell me anything about his plan until just before the game when he just sent me out to make a presentation to the Russians. And this time I had a bit of revenge, because I gave them flowers. . . .'

The result of the game also gave Rangers revenge for the missed penalty by Manager Waddell which robbed them of victory twenty-five years before. It was the goal which decided the game that brought that signpost for the future that I mentioned earlier. Because the goal that won the game was scored by the golden head of wonder boy centre-forward Derek Johnstone . . . the same boy who had won them the League Cup and who was later to earn them a replay of the Scottish Cup Final. Johnstone, the boy from Dundee, who makes a habit of scoring goals on the big occasions. . . .

Here Johnstone recalls that game against the Russians:

'I wasn't even born when the first game was played between the two teams but being in Glasgow and around the club you couldn't help but hear all the stories about that first match. By the time the game came along we all realised that it had been a very important milestone in the history of the club . . . and we wanted to get a victory.

'Of course, it was a very new experience for me. The occasion wasn't as big as it had been in the League Cup Final when I had faced Celtic but this was the first time I had been picked to play a full game against Continental opposition. I had appeared for a very short time against Bayern Munich at Ibrox but before that the only taste of European football I'd had live was a European Cup semi-final in my home town of Dundee when Milan came to Dens Park to play Dundee.

'Right away the Russians struck me as being a well-disciplined side. They played a little bit the way that the Russian international team plays when you see them in action on television. They were methodical, sticking closely to their playing system, and having the same attitude as ourselves to things like tackling.

'In certain ways I did find it harder to play against them as compared to a normal Scottish side. They had a zonal system of marking which they used and which was particularly effective. Normally in this country you find yourself being marked by the same man all the time during a game and you get used to trying to slip the man and make space for yourself. You reckon you have succeeded when he isn't around and you

The moment that brought so many memories to life for the fans and
for Rangers' one-time skipper Jock Shaw. The man who captained
the Ibrox team in the first game against Moscow Dynamo leaves the
field before the start of the game at Ibrox after a midfield
presentation. Shaw is on the right of the picture, accompanied by
former opponent Beskov (centre) and Lev Yashin (left)

A portrait of Derek Johnstone, the youngster whose goal beat
Dynamo in the Ibrox return clash

collect the ball. But with Dynamo if you moved away from one man, say, in my case, the centre-half, then I found someone else picking me up immediately. It's not so easy to find space when they are using this system against you . . . especially when they stick to it as strictly as the Russians did.

'The Dynamo team we met that night at Ibrox was particularly strong in midfield where they had a couple of outstanding players in Maslov and Zhukov. They were the ideal types for the vital area in the middle of the park. They could win the ball and when they had possession they could use it too. They were strong, powerful players who seemed to be back helping their defence whenever they were in trouble and up backing their forwards when they had moved into attack against us. They were stronger than we were that night in midfield and as a result most of our attacks had to come via the wings. That led to a great night for Willie Henderson. He had a sensational game and set up a lot of chances for me in the air. This was one department, too, where the Russians were anything but strong. They just didn't have any great heading ability.

'I found it surprising that their centre-half or their "sweeper" didn't challenge me at all to start with. They seemed perfectly content to let me get up there and make contact while he tried to position himself for where he expected my header to go.

'It was only later in the game that he tried to jump with me and he just didn't go up the way that a centre-half at home would go up. He didn't have the same aggression as most defenders in Scotland show and so I was able to win most of the balls in the air that night . . . including the one that brought the goal and the result that we had wanted so much.

'It is such a different game, though, when you face up to these Continental teams. You can feel that you are making out all right against teams at home in Scotland and then you can be thrown out of gear by a team from Europe simply because they do things that you don't anticipate and may never have encountered before. The older players tell me that when you come up against different teams from different countries then you keep on learning something new on specific aspects of the game. The Spaniards and the other Latin countries have players who can shield the ball well, then the Germans have another style and the Iron Curtain countries another . . . and always you can learn and improve from the experience.

112   'The Russian idea of not having a defender challenge too

often in the air suited me. I suppose that I have made any reputation I have so far by scoring goals with my head. Yet when I was a schoolboy I didn't reckon that heading was my best feature. It just seems to have developed that way since I turned senior with the Rangers. Because of this I try to watch as many players who are good in the air as possible. I admire the three Welsh strikers in particular, John Toshack, Wyn Davies and Ron Davies. The one I like most is Toshack of Liverpool who is good in the air and also seems able to take up position very dangerously any time I catch him on the telly. He makes goods runs into position and this is something that I know I have to improve on.

'It may seem strange but when I look back on my twin tastes of European football I rate the Dynamo team ahead of Bayern.

'I know that we beat the Russians and could only draw with Bayern at Ibrox but that doesn't change my opinion any. I thought that the Russians seemed better-balanced and if they had had a reasonable striker then they might have made things harder for us than they did. They weren't well-equipped to get goals while Bayern, of course, always have Gerd Muller lying around to snap up any chances. But in the midfield they were far ahead of the Germans in my view.

'The great memory of the game for me will be that goal, and the result, and maybe, too, the surprise that the Russians showed when they were told I was only seventeen. But if the memory of our game lasts as long as the memory of the first then I reckon all of us at Ibrox will be happy.'

And, of course, it seems certain that the memory will live on. Perhaps the match will not be so celebrated as that first one because of the changing circumstances of the game where European football is so readily available now. But it could be that in the future the friendship of the two clubs, one from Glasgow, one from Moscow, will be strengthened by yet another game. When that happens then you can take it that Derek Johnstone's headed goal in 1970 will be remembered along with the fabled happenings of 1945.

Rangers' iron man and skipper John Greig, the man the Ibrox club relied upon in their lean years

Hampden belonged to the Rangers' Fans

THE abiding memory for myself and for so many of the other Rangers' players and officials when we look back to our two epic Scottish Cup Final clashes with Celtic last season will not be the goal by Derek Johnstone which earned us a replay, nor even the injuries that haunted us on the long road to Hampden. . . .

Instead, our memory will be of the fans who packed the Rangers' end of the towering terracings of Hampden. I know that I will never be able to forget them for the way that they supported us in both the games, and above all for the way they stood their ground at the end of the second game, after we had lost the Cup that they were so certain we were going to win. In every other Old Firm match in my memory the end of the ground which houses the fans of the defeated team is normally empty as soon as the final whistle is blown. And the usual reception for the beaten Old Firm team in a Cup final is the jeers of the rival support . . . because they are the only fans who have stayed. But this last time, as we stood on the edge of the Hampden pitch that night in May, watching Celtic collect their winners' medals we suddenly realised that besides the victory songs from the jubilant Celtic end, there were our songs and chants, too. The fans there were still cheering for us and they remained there to give us a special roar as we collected the medals for the runners-up. As far as I was concerned Hampden belonged to them that night. . . .

That attitude typified the spirit that they had shown right through our Cup run and especially in the tense one hundred and eighty minutes of Cup Final drama against Celtic. They had seen us go behind in the first game—even though it was so dreadfully against the run of play—and then go two goals down in the first half of the replay and all the time they backed us solidly. Their loyalty was tremendous and the urge that they gave to us couldn't have been bettered by fans anywhere else in the world.

And, when you think back to the weeks preceding that two-match Final you couldn't have blamed them so very much if they had been shouted down and even out-numbered by the Celtic fans at these Hampden games. Nothing had gone right for us in these weeks while Celtic had clinched the League title after suffering some anxious moments as Aberdeen led for so long, and now the men from Parkhead were being tipped by everyone to add the Scottish Cup to that amazing sixth-in-a-row title success. In that sense, in the way the talk was going, in the way the players of other clubs and the bookies felt, it was very similar to the prelude to the League Cup Final, which, of course, we had won. Only, this time, to add to form worries we had been hit and hit hard by a series of injury blows. Not the simple little knocks that took a day or two, or even a week or two to clear up. Not a twist or a strain or a bruise which could be put right by intensive treatment right up to the day of the Final. No. We were hit by a hat-trick of serious injuries just as we were preparing ourselves for that run-in at the end of the long, gruelling season. These were injuries that couldn't possibly heal in time and they were added to the bumps and bruises that a team always gathers as the season nears it's climax.

The first of the three happened at training during a practice game at the Albion. We only had a few minutes left in the kick-about that we usually end training with when our link man or 'sweeper' Dave Smith went down in a heap after a tackle and we found that he had broken his ankle. It was a dreadful moment for all of us that morning at the Albion. After all, it had been a year almost to the day that Dave had suffered a broken leg in a Rugby Park League game against Kilmarnock. Now, here he was again, with another fracture, and another heart-breaking end to his season while Hampden and a Cup Final appearance loomed so close for us all. Dave, my room-mate on any trips that Rangers made abroad, had worked so hard and so well to get back into the team. He had helped us to beat Aberdeen, his old club, in the Cup game at Ibrox and now here he was out again.

It is hard, even now, to describe just how badly we all felt about that accident.

Well, there's an old saying that these things come in threes and, right enough, that's the way it happened for Rangers. Just as Hampden approached we lost two more of our young first team stars. First of all our brilliant right-back Sandy Jardine suffered a hair-line fracture of his leg in a League game against Cowdenbeath at Central Park. At first none of us realised that it was a serious injury. But, it was. Sandy had his leg put in plaster and the player who had been probably the most improved player in Scottish soccer last season was suddenly a part of our Hampden hoodoo. Instead of lining up in his normal position against Celtic in the Final Sandy was destined to be limping along to watch the game from the stand on crutches.

Joining him as a spectator, and also on crutches, was midfield babe Alfie Conn. This time the injury blow hit us just seven days before we were due to meet the Celtic. We were playing a Glasgow Cup game against Queens Park at Hampden, a game that Manager Willie Waddell had shrewdly arranged to keep us in condition and also allow us to get the feel of the Cup Final pitch. You see, there had been a two-week gap between our last League game and the Final and this was the ideal chance to keep playing on what would otherwise have been a blank Saturday. Still, there was no escaping the jinx. Alfie Conn went off the field in the second-half with a knee injury. At first a cartilage operation looked as if it might be necessary but eventually the trouble was diagnosed as badly damaged ligaments. Still, even that second opinion didn't give Alfie a ghost of a chance of making an appearance in the final. So that was the situation we were in as the game approached us. Injuries were making sure that the player pool at Ibrox was being stretched to the limit . . . and even in the last few days there were more worries.

You see, besides the bad injuries, there were three more players receiving treatment in a bid to have them fit for the game. This trio was made up of Willie Nathieson, Colin Jackson and wee Willie Henderson. Wee Willie was so serious a doubt that the Boss had him leave his own home in Airdrie and move to Edinburgh to have special treatment and training in secret in an attempt to have the outside-right ready to play at Hampden. It worked and the wee man did play but the worry hung over the fans all week that the injury jinx would hit us again right on the eve of the game.

Somehow, though, even with the knowledge that we were going to have to face a Celtic team who had come clear of injuries and who, in fact, had hit their best form towards the end of the season didn't worry any of us too much. We accepted that we were going into the game without three experienced and good players but not one of the players seemed to allow

117

A series of four pictures to show the kind of power and inspiration that Greig contributes to Rangers. They were taken in the first round Scottish Cup tie against Falkirk at Ibrox, the tie which acted as a launching pad for Rangers to reach the Hampden final

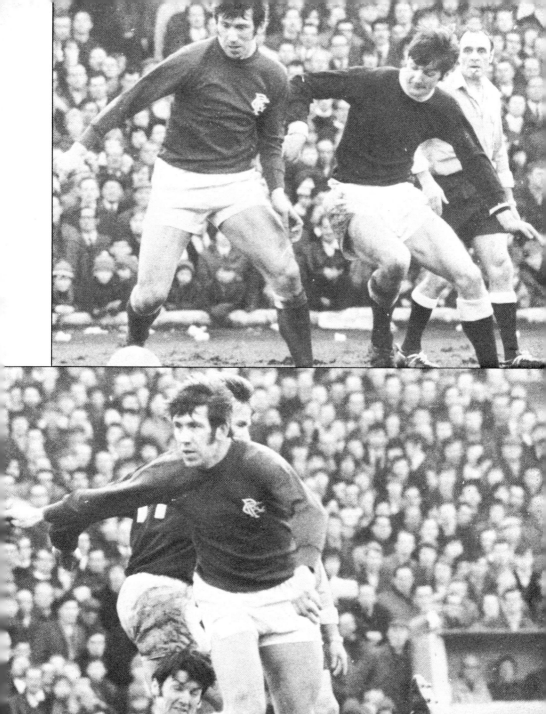

himself to get over-anxious about this.

I don't know why it was, but we all stayed remarkably calm considering the situation. Probably it was because we realised that the players who would be stepping into the first team to take over from the injured men were experienced and not the type who would be over-awed by the occasion. There was Andy Penman, for instance, a player who had played so often in big games, and at full-back there was Alec Miller who had done so well as our regular left-back earlier in the season. We had Derek Johnstone around, too, the kid whose goal had won us the League Cup the last time we had come to Hampden in a Cup Final. And against, Celtic, too! With all of this going through our minds and also a bit of an aggrieved feeling, I reckon, because no one gave us an earthly chance of winning the game and stopping Celtic's march to the League and Cup double, we were keyed up for the match when it finally arrived.

We felt that we could still win and the manager, Mr. Waddell, had exactly the same idea as every player. In spite of the views of so many people before the game there was never the slightest chance of us going out to defend in this game. Some caution might have been justified when considering the injuries but the Boss was very conscious of the fact that this was the Scottish Cup Final, a showpiece game for our football, and so he sent us out to have a go at Celtic. We forgot our troubles. We left them behind us in the dressing room and decided to carry the game to Celtic. The Boss felt that we were a better team going forward and that's how we played against our Old Firm rivals. We played to win that game and to win that Cup. In the end it didn't work out that way . . . but we won a moral victory and even the Celtic fans in the 120,000 crowd at Hampden would probably agree with me when I say that. The only reason we didn't take the Cup back to Ibrox that Saturday was because we missed chances. In that first-half we tore huge gaps in the Celtic defence but we simply could not put the ball in the net. Celtic could. And they did. Bobby Lennox, who has scored so often against us in these Old Firm games, jetted through our defence to put them a goal ahead towards the end of the first half.

It was an injustice. We seethed at it in the dressing room at half-time and we knew now that we had a job on our hands if we were to win the game. Celtic had survived all our pressure, had had lucky escapes around their goal and then had broken upfield to score. It was all going their way and we had to reverse that trend. Of course, we still had an ace up our sleeves . . . our teenage centre-forward Derek Johnstone. He came on as a substitute midway through the second-half to replace Andy Penman. Then, right on the final whistle he moved through between Celtic goalkeeper Evan Williams and their wing-half George Connelly and headed the ball over the 'keeper's head and into the net. It rolled towards that line so slowly but Derek knew it was a goal all the way. He turned to take the applause of the fans before he even saw it cross the line.

It was unbelievable that he should have done it again, score a goal at Hampden in a Cup Final, I mean. A few months earlier he had won us the League Cup with a header. Now here he was with another Hampden header earning us a replay in the Scottish Cup Final! It was too late for Celtic to hit back, too late for us to make up any further for the chances that we had missed and so we had won the right of a replay on the following Wednesday night. It was wonderful for Derek but I couldn't help wondering if he was going to make things hard for himself . . . or, at least, if the fans might now set too high standards for him. He is potentially a great player and quite brilliant in the air. I can't remember anyone else beating the Celtic centre-half Billy McNeil quite so often in the air as Derek did in these matches he played against him. All I hope is that the fans remember that he is young, that he has a lot of time to keep scoring goals for Rangers and that they will be kind to him if he hits a lean spell.

Anyhow, he had made up all so happy at that final whistle. The Cup was still a possibility for us. That was the big thing as we crowded into the dressing room . . . but the cost of that match had still to be counted.

That night after the game Alec Miller came into the banquet which had been arranged, win or lose, by the club, and told us that he had broken his jaw. Alec, who had done so well in place of Sandy Jardine, had been injured fairly early in the game in a collision with Celtic left-back Jim Brogan. He had had double vision and had been in some pain but typically he had insisted on playing on. It was only when he went for an X-ray that night after the game that he discovered he had sustained a double fracture of the jaw. The pain must have been terrible during the game but he hadn't admitted that to any of us. Courageously he had decided to stay on the field . . . but even courage couldn't have him ready for the replay. The hoodoo had struck once more. . . .

Skipper John Greig is the Ranger
on the ground in this melee during
the first of the Scottish Cup Final
clashes with Celtic. The other
players from left to right are Jim
Craig (Celtic), Billy McNeill
(Celtic), Colin Stein (Rangers)
and bringing the ball under
control, Jimmy Johnstone (Celtic)

Ronnie McKinnon and Colin Jackson are the Rangers' attackers in this goal-mouth incident from the Cup tie at Ibrox where Rangers beat the holders Aberdeen. It was eventually this type of move which led to Jackson scoring the goal. The Aberdeen players in the picture from left to right are, goalkeeper Bobby Clark, centre-half Tommy McMillan and right-back Henning Boel

Once again it was not a simple injury to a player, the kind you expect, at times, and can shake off in a day or two. By the time Wednesday night came along Alec Miller would have gone through an operation in a Glasgow hospital and another full-back had to be found to take his place.

The depth and the value of the player pool at Ibrox had been demonstrated for that first game. Despite the injuries to important players we had gone out and shown the fans the same flair for Cup football that we had shown in all our ties last year. In fact, we should have won the Cup that first time round . . . now, though, we were in a situation where almost any player pool would have been stretched beyond its limits. We had FOUR members of the first team pool out of the replay and somewhere, somehow, within ninety-six hours, the Boss had to produce a right-back who would be capable both of facing Celtic and reacting without nerves to the prospect of a hundred thousand crowd at Hampden.

We all had our own ideas on what might happen for the return game on Wednesday. I reckoned myself, for instance, that the Boss would plump for a team reshuffle with either yours truly or Colin Jackson going to the right-back problem spot where both of us had played before. That would have let Derek Johnstone come into the team from the start with Andy Penman and Alec MacDonald teaming up in midfield. By the time Wednesday came along I had just about convinced myself that this was going to happen. But the manager had his own ideas. He decided that he did not want to chop and change a team which had blended so well in the first match simply to solve the problem of one position. He made up his mind that one player would be called into the team to take over from Alec Miller and that the rest of us would stay as we were, with Derek Johnstone staying on the substitute's bench again at the start of the game.

No one in the team knew who would be playing in the right-back position until we were in the Hampden dressing room forty minutes before the kick off. Then the bombshell choice which was to shock the more than one hundred thousand fans in Hampden was announced . . . Mr. Waddell had plucked yet another youngster from the reserve team to do the job in the final. The player he had picked was 21-old-year Jim Denny who had signed for Rangers about four months earlier and who had played only around eight games or so in the reserve team. He had been a wing-half in these appearances but the

Boss had seen potential and so he played his first first-team game, and his first-ever match as a right back, in the final of the Scottish Cup. It must have worried the fans yet again, and even now it must still make some of you raise your eyebrows a little.

Yet, quite honestly, I wasn't too worried by the selection. There was something about Jim, something about him that I had noticed on his first day at training, which gave me confidence in him at that moment. He had arrived at Ibrox full of beans, the kind of youngster with a bit of devil in him and from that first time I remembered him I had the feeling that this was the type of player you could depend on never to get too nervous. And, quite honestly, before we went out to play in that game, it wasn't the occasion nor the fact that he was going out to face Celtic, nor even the huge crowd, which worried him. All he was concerned about was whether he would let the rest of us down or not. Well, he didn't. He stuck to the job he had been given, showing flashes of coolness that many much more experienced players do not show in an Old Firm game . . . and he came out of that ninety minutes with a lot of credit.

We lost the game and with it we lost the Scottish Cup, possibly because our attitude had changed a little bit by the time we approached that replay.

We had gone into that first game determined to prove to the world that we were as good a team as Celtic even though we had been crippled by injuries. It is just possible that when we went into the second game we had been heartened too much by that performance on Saturday. Perhaps some of us thought that it was going to be like that first match all over again, with us able to dominate the play and force the game in the way we wanted it to go. It didn't turn out like that.

Celtic played well and we didn't hit the form that we had reached the first time around. They scored twice inside three minutes in the first half. Lou Macari, a new face for the replay, grabbed the first and then Harry Hood scored the second from a penalty after Ronnie McKinnon had brought down Jimmy Johnstone in the box. We did get one back in the second-half when Derek Johnstone—yes, again—panicked the Celtic defence and their right-back Jim Craig turned the ball into his own net. But though that goal gave us a lift it was not enough and we finished up losing the Cup that we had all thought we were going to win. Right through some of our poorer Leagues games we had sustained ourselves with the thought that at the end of the year we would be lifting the Scottish Cup and that would make up for everything. We had played really well in all the games in the Cup but, at the end, we hit these injuries, missed the chances in the first game and then faded a little in the second. It was a bitter disappointment to me, personally, because I had wanted to lead Rangers to a victory in one of the major trophies, especially as I had had to sit out the League Cup win because of illness.

Still, there can be a next time. The fans stayed with us and that helped me and the rest of the lads get over the disappointment. We're sure that with supporters like these we can do anything. . . .

They proved themselves the best in the business that night at Hampden, the night that the great Glasgow ground belonged to them in defeat.